PRAISE FOR DARRIN HAGEN...

WITH BELLS ON

"*With Bells On* is flat-out wonderful."
—Stephen Hunt, *Calgary Herald*

"I'm still laughing after seeing *With Bells On* last night at the Red Barn Theatre, truly one of the funniest plays I've seen in a long time."
—Joanna Brady, *KONK Life Key West*

THE EDMONTON QUEEN

"Hagen has the gift of gab. And he tells us a bizarre, humane story in extravagant, mock heroic, hothouse language that seems as right as red lipstick for the occasion. Unmissable."
—Liz Nicholls, *Edmonton Journal*

THE EMPRESS & THE PRIME MINISTER

"With this show, Hagen has matured into a beautifully balanced playwright/ performer. He has accomplished one of theatre's most difficult tasks - to have his audience walk away with a much greater understanding – intellectually, emotionally, intuitively – of his theme, having told his tale in an easily digestible, entertaining way, using all of the dramatic tools at his disposal."
—Graham Hicks, *hicksbiz.com*

THE

CROWN

COLLECTION

THE CROWN

COLLECTION

Plays by

DARRIN
HAGEN

NeWest
Press

Title: The Crown Collection : Plays / by Darrin Hagen.

Names: Hagen, Darrin, 1964- author. |
Container of (work): Hagen, Darrin, 1964- With Bells On. |
Container of (work): Hagen, Darrin, 1964- The Edmonton Queen (Play). |
Container of (work): Hagen, Darrin, 1964- The Empress & The Prime Minister.
Series: Prairie Play Series ; 35.
Description: Series statement: Prairie Play Series ; 35
Identifiers: Canadiana (print) 20260159433 |
Canadiana (ebook) 20260160660 | ISBN 9781774391426
(softcover) | ISBN 9781774391433 (EPUB)
Subjects: LCGFT: Drama. | LCGFT: Autobiographical drama.
Classification: LCC PS8615.A36 C76 2026 | DDC C812/.6—dc23
Classification: LCC PS8626.U7515 N36 2026 | DDC C813/.6—dc23

Editor for the Press: Leslie Vermeer
Cover Design: Christine Hassay-Kohler
Interior Design: Meredith Thompson
Cover Photo: Ryan Parker, Ryan Parker Photography
Interior photos: Ian Jackson / EPIC Photography

The poetry excerpts that appear in *The Edmonton Queen* are by Stephen Dyson. Cover crown donated by Empress XV, Twiggy.

NeWest Press wishes to acknowledge that the land on which we operate is Treaty 6 territory and a traditional meeting ground and home for many Indigenous Peoples, including Cree, Saulteaux, Niitsitapi (Blackfoot), Métis, Dene, and Nakota Sioux since time immemorial. ||

NeWest Press acknowledges the support of the Canada Council for the Arts, the Government of Alberta through the Ministry of Arts, Culture and Status of Women, and the Edmonton Arts Council for support of our publishing program. This project is funded in part by the Government of Canada.

NeWest Press
10131 97 Street
Edmonton, Alberta T5J 0L2
780.432.9427
www.newestpress.com

Printed and bound in Canada.

CONTENTS

CONTENT ADVISORY: While I have done all I can to update the writing to reflect our growing awareness and pursuit of inclusion, respect, and equality, some outdated terminology remains, retained consciously to reflect the period in which these plays emerged.

INTRODUCTION

STEP ONE is to write what you know.

Except it isn't. Step one is to live a life worth writing about.

I remember in alarming detail the frantic pounding of my heart as I rode the #5 bus along Jasper Avenue on a cold and dark January rush hour in 1983. I sat at the back of the crowded bus, a box in my lap with the Tallcrest Shoes logo on it. I was on my way to my apartment to practise walking in those shoes: size thirteen black patent open-toed slingbacks. My first show on an Edmonton stage in drag was two weeks away. What lay ahead was impossible to know, or even imagine, but on January 14, 1983, Gloria Hole was born. (In truth, she had been there my entire life — but that night I finally stepped out of her way.)

Sixteen months after that first drag show on the legendary Flashback stage, a crown was placed on my head. I'll never truly understand the inevitability of that moment. But it *was* inevitable.

My years as a drag artiste in Edmonton's underground have been a constant supply of inspiration for my writing. That singular act — stepping into those giant shoes and never looking back — drew me into an experience that forever altered how I see the world. Every time I write about drag, or create a drag character for the stage, that intense decade of discovery, infatuation, obsession, and ambition drives every word.

The Crown Collection celebrates that era of my own evolution: the years when Gloria was in charge of my life. It showcases three very different approaches to drag artistry, and could also be said to represent a writer at three different stages of life and career — as well as my personal feelings about drag.

The Edmonton Queen is my dream come to life — a young me diving headfirst into a fabulous circus with no clue of the darkness ahead. *With Bells On* is a more jaded and world-weary me, still overcoming my doubts and fears, but with the reflection and pain central to the comedy. Finally, *The Empress & The Prime Minister* draws a picture of a more defiant Queen: drag as a political act, a sacrificial self-othering in an attempt to transform the world.

The three plays also represent very different styles and approaches to writing. I call *The Edmonton Queen* a hyper-epic fairy-tale memoir. I didn't invent the story — I just had to breathe life into it. My first real piece of writing, it's audacious and extravagant, using titles and alliterations and Capital Letters with abandon. I have never written anything like it since. *With Bells On*, while poised on the possibility of truth, is pure invention, and even though the themes and experiences in the play are drawn from my own, I have, thankfully, never been stuck in an elevator in drag. Yet. Finally, *The Empress & The Prime Minister* uses a verbatim approach to play construction encompassing political archives, Queer history archives, and my own insights into drag activism, mixed with informed speculation.

For each of these Queens/characters, being a drag artiste isn't just a costume. It's a recognition of destiny. My goal has always been to dig down underneath the makeup and reveal the humans behind these glamorous creations.

With Bells On

THIS PLAY didn't start its life as a Christmas play, or even as a play in an elevator.

I was hosting a staged reading in Edmonton when I saw James Hamilton on the stage. For some reason my mind went directly to *Would he ever look hilarious standing next to me while I'm in full drag.* I probably even mentioned that to him that evening, and that I wanted to write a play that would exploit that hilarity.

I pictured two neighbours living on the same floor of an apartment building: one a flamboyant drag queen, the other a very square and conservative man in a suit. That's all I knew. I started writing but it didn't take long before I was stuck. One day, as the notorious elevator in my high-rise clunked to a rough stop on the ground floor, my friend Neon quipped, "You should write a play about this scary elevator." That gave me a unique situation to explore. I ended with ten maybe-funny pages, and I took advantage of the new play development program offered by Lunchbox Theatre's Stage One Festival of New Canadian Work (then sponsored by Suncor) and submitted my scribblings.

Dramaturge Caroline Russell-King must have seen something in those pages because it wasn't long before I was having a meeting with her to discuss possible directions for the play, and a full draft was commissioned by Lunchbox Theatre.

I have been on many elevators in drag. It's never fun. I'm out of my element, trapped in an artificial closeness with people that I would normally never encounter while I'm dressed like that. I usually stare straight ahead and wait for it to end. I've ridden fifteen floors with Joe, the redneck neighbour, off to the rigs at four a.m. after his night at the strip club. I've ridden with groups of seniors dragging their IV poles out to the parking lot for a smoke. Once I was in a mirrored elevator, and so (through giant Jackie O sunglasses) I watched the reflection of every other person silently gawking at me, not realizing I could see them staring. At nearly seven feet tall in heels, there's no mistaking me for anything but what I am. So the character of Natasha is a bit of an Ice Maiden, to keep the curious at bay. Natasha's height is important. She's in no danger in that elevator. She just wants to get back to a place where she feels she can be herself. She has zero intention of opening up about her life to this stranger.

But the character of Ted was different. I wanted to avoid the tired trope of the straight guy being all freaked out by the encounter, or being fooled by the disguise. And so I made him curious, but not in a creepy way. He has to be someone the audience roots for. It feels like Natasha's story at first because she and her costume and her monologues take up so much room. But it's Ted who experiences transformation and change. It's his journey towards a more exciting life.

During the Lunchbox Theatre Stage One workshop, the piece evolved. Russell-King and director Ian Prinsloo had lots of questions. It was Ian who asked a very pointed question about a stage direction that indicated the drag queen's noisy and tinkly entrance. It said, *She is covered in sparkles and bows, like a Christmas tree.* Ian asked why the Queen was dressed like a Christmas tree.

"Well, I didn't mean that literally. I was just trying to be funny and descriptive. I mean, what Queen in her right mind would go out dressed as a Christmas tree? Unless ...?" And then I recalled the annual Christmas Queen pageant in Edmonton. And suddenly the entire reason for the play opened before me. I, who was not a fan of the holidays at all, was writing my first Christmas play.

With Bells On opened at Calgary's Lunchbox Theatre in 2010, starring Stafford Perry as Ted and Paul Welch as Natasha (filling the elevator from floor to ceiling at seven feet tall in headdress and heels — costume designed by Norman J. MacDonald, who had the good fortune to be working at a Christmas decoration boutique at the time), and I'll confess that the riotous and enthusiastic response to the claustrophobic journey of Ted and Natasha caught me completely by surprise. It was nominated for a Betty Mitchell Award for Best New Play, and tall and strapping actor Paul Welch won the award for Best Actor in a Musical or Comedy for his sparkling and vulnerable portrayal of Natasha.

In 2011, my own company, Guys In Disguise, produced the comedy as part of the Roxy Series at Theatre Network, with Paul Welch reprising his role as Natasha, and the very funny James Hamilton finally inhabiting the role of Ted that I had created with him in mind. The play felt a bit short, and so I added the car-and-police-chase monologue for Natasha (a true story that I had always wanted to find a home for).

The show was nominated for Sterling awards for Outstanding New Play, Outstanding Independent Production, and Outstanding

Costume Design. It played again in 2012 and 2013, becoming something of a Roxy Theatre holiday staple for many.

In 2013 it was produced by Ireland's Athlone Little Theatre as their entry into the Ireland One-Act Drama Competition and played in cities around Ireland — the first of my plays to ever be seen in Europe. It was directed by Oliver Hegarty and starred Martin Kelleher and Declan Finn. It was revisited later that year in Athlone, Ireland, for the holidays.

The Guys In Disguise production saw a remount in 2014 with the original Calgary cast at Lunchbox Theatre, where it sold out by opening night and was held over. On closing night of the Calgary run, actor Paul Welch had played the role of Natasha more than one hundred times over five seasons. Stafford Perry was nominated for Best Actor in a Comedy, and the production won a Calgary Critics' Award for Best Remount.

In 2016 it was produced by New Vintage Theatre in Kelowna, British Columbia, directed by Bonnie Gratz and Logan Mullin. The role of Ted was played by Zachary Richard Fox, and Natasha was played by Kelowna drag performer Shannon Lester (aka Sasha Zamolodchikova), whose mom flew all the way from Newfoundland for the opening.

In 2018, *With Bells On* received its American premiere as Christopher Peterson, my drag sister, female impersonator and drag artiste extraordinaire, directed and designed the play at the Red Barn Theatre in Key West, Florida, starring Trey Gerrald as Natasha and Don Bearden as Ted. Christopher asked me to expand the play and suggested a story he knew from my past — being dressed as a mermaid while being taunted by preschoolers (my most humiliating drag experience, all caught on video for posterity). I cracked the play open one more time and added another monologue for Natasha.

At an after-party in Key West, Trey told me how clever it was that I had named the character Natasha. I asked why. He replied, "Well, because of what it means." He saw my puzzled look and so pressed on: "Natasha means 'born on Christmas.'" I swear I had no idea until then. (I was thinking Boris and Natasha from the Rocky and Bullwinkle cartoons because Natasha is the tall one).

Guys In Disguise remounted the play in 2019 at the Varscona Theatre with Hamilton reprising his role as Ted, and another extremely tall Natasha hit the stage portrayed by actor Jake Tkaczyk.

In 2023, a musical adaptation that had been in the works for two years by Devanand Janki and composer Tommy Newman for New York City's Live and In Color made its world premiere at the newly rebuilt Theatre Network starring rising drag star Zachary Parsons-Lozinski (aka Lilith Fair) as Natasha and Thomas Jones as Ted. Suddenly my little elevator play had a huge revolving set, a full band, and songs. *With Bells On! The Musical* received two Sterling nominations for Outstanding Musical Score and Outstanding Musical Director.

At the same time in Calgary, Lunchbox Theatre revived the play again, partly in solidarity with Calgary's drag community as it was being besieged by right-wing extremists. The young all-Queer company production resulted in acting nominations for both Bernardo Pacheco as Ted and Joel Schaefer as Natasha.

In 2024, fourteen years after it began, it received its second U.S. production by Richmond Triangle Players in Richmond, Virginia, starring local drag legend Wette Midler as Natasha and Doug Schneider as Ted. One of my favourite things about other artists interpreting the script is the delightful moment when I see a photo of the costumes that have been created for Natasha. In Richmond, Natasha's giant gold bell boobs, designed by Alex Valentine, rank high on my list of favourites.

One strange tidbit about *With Bells On* is that it's a role I wrote for myself, and yet in many years of productions, I have never performed in it. I've watched some brilliant performers chew up the scenery in the role of Natasha — and I experience no envy. Just joy. It's been the best Christmas present ever. Every person who has played a part in this play has influenced it, and so a debt of gratitude is due. So many gifted imaginations and ideas merged; no wonder its appeal seems so universal.

With Bells On is for all the people who don't get drawn into the mania of the holidays, who don't hum along to the Christmas carols that blast through tinny speakers starting in November, and who, frankly, don't have the time for Christmas because there's just too much work to do. This play is for anyone who was left out of holiday celebrations because they didn't fit in. When people who are strangers end up sharing time together, even though they are worlds apart — that's the real magic of the season.

The Edmonton Queen

IN THE wake of the plague decade, AIDS continued to ravage my community through the 1990s. The growing body count compelled me to write down some of the stories of the vanishing royal sisterhood and the mythical family trees they had created. I wanted there to be something left other than faded glamour shots and broken, rusty tiaras. I could literally feel history erasing us.

I preferred to focus mostly on the parts covered in rhinestones and crowns.

I had written very little up to that point. But I could tell stories. True ones. Wild ones. Stories no one would believe. Every story started as a eulogy. I created some stories to share at funerals, or in memoriam, a way of keeping their memories alive. I was finally discovering, for the very first time, what it meant to write about something I was passionate about.

A society was vanishing, dying in a manner that was as needless as it was poetic. Someone had to record it — while there was still time. Not only to remember and to preserve, but to celebrate the lives cut short.

As the bodies piled up, so did the stories.

I fell in love with words and how they could move people. And how they could turn a gaggle of drag queens (an embarrassment of bitches) into tragic heroes.

I kept writing — fearlessly, with a flair for the dramatic hyperbole that only *The Edmonton Queen* could possess. Ron Jenkins took on the job of guiding the stories to the stage as director and dramaturge.

Deciding to do a one-person show is the most arrogant decision an artist can make. And getting through the first performance is the most humbling thing that will ever happen to that artist. Not realizing this until it was too late, I put it onstage.

The first version of *The Edmonton Queen: Not a Riverboat Story* made its debut at the 1996 Edmonton Fringe and was held over at Theatre Network. Since it's really a Throne Speech, I had snagged a throne from the First Night Festival and repainted it. Mz. Flashback 15 Mandy Kamp provided silhouette impersonations of the Queens in the story while I delivered the monologue. During the run of the play, publisher Candas Jane Dorsey came backstage after the show and asked if I had more stories, then told me I should write a book. A year later, that book was launched by Slipstream Books.

But the play resurfaced in 2000. And when I started to memorize it, I realized I had all this new material from the book that I couldn't ignore and so I rewrote the play. It was a humble little show — just me, the throne, a silver dress, and a disco ball. This newer, more confident version (now titled *The Edmonton Queen*) began at First Night Festival (Y2K 2000) and then toured to Regina's Globe Theatre and the Winnipeg Fringe Festival. And in 2001 that version returned to the Edmonton Fringe. The list of names of departed Queens grew longer with every production. The blue throne rode in the back of a rental truck across the prairies and back.

After that, I always thought I'd never do the play again, that I had outgrown it. In 2006 I was approached by Ruth Linka of Brindle and Glass Publishing to develop a tenth-anniversary edition of the book. During the preparation for that edition, I learned that Lulu LaRude had brain cancer. Those final chapters are laced with mourning because we both knew what was coming. There was no joy in creating that edition ... just lots of reckoning. But in 2007, as I held the new edition in my hands, I thought, *Finally ... it's done.*

But then in 2009 I was approached by Thomas Scott of Fringe Theatre Adventures to perform it one more time. I said no several times. Revisiting the play scared me, because the sad list of names now included the grand Queen who had been the living inspiration for the story. I wasn't sure I could even say those words aloud, let alone on a stage with an audience watching. But I'm so glad I did, because that production, directed by Gina Moe, was the most glorious and sparkling version yet. Lulu would have been so proud. The new improved throne, designed by Robert Shannon, dwarfed even *this* Glamazon, and under dazzling lighting by Roger Schultz, the production was a fitting end to what has easily been the most intense and emotional (and enduring) writing experience I will undergo in this lifetime.

The Edmonton Queen became my calling card, my unofficial title in the media, and my nickname. It's the project that launched me, changed me, and lingers with me decades later. For me it's the proof that authenticity triumphs. I didn't really write it. It was a gift.

All I had to do was remember.

Like I could ever forget.

The closing paragraphs of this Throne Speech still make me cry. Every time.

The Empress & The Prime Minister

IN 2013 my husband and I flew to Toronto. (I could say husband because we had finally gotten married a week earlier after decades of living in sin.) I was to be inducted into the Q Hall of Fame Canada. I still have no idea who put my name forward, but I'm so grateful for that evening, because while listening to the speakers that night, I was reintroduced to Mr. ted northe: The Empress of Canada.

I had met ted decades earlier, ever so briefly, because he was a figurehead in the North American drag world. I was Imperial Crown Princess in Edmonton (to Empress IX Lulu LaRude, of course), and my star was rising through the drag scene. Somehow, ted and I had both survived the 1980s. And now I was watching him give a stirring and shattering keynote address at the Q Hall of Fame event in Toronto.

That night, he shared the moving and emotional story of his early years as a drag activist in the 1950s and '60s in Canada and the U.S. Partway through his speech I leaned over and whispered to my husband, "His story should be turned into a play."

It was real life, but it had all the elements of an exciting script: a pioneer who found himself at a crossroads in history, poised to change the world. The fact that he had decided decades ago to do that as a gay man in a dress just made the tale more compelling.

Mr. northe passed away a few short months later. The speech I had witnessed was in fact his final time addressing the community he had worked so hard to liberate. The national press told bits of the story of northe and his work with Prime Minister Pierre Trudeau, culminating in the partial decriminalization of homosexuality in 1969 with the passing of Bill C-150. In the North American drag community, members of the International Court System mourned the loss of one of their founders, and tireless advocates.

I learned later that his friend Paul Therien had filmed several hours of interviews with ted before his death. Paul graciously shared those interviews with me and soon I was madly transcribing hours of video. The stories he told in those interviews became the spine of this play.

As I wrote, the fiftieth anniversary of Bill C-150 was approaching, and I wanted to be able to commemorate that moment, and ted's pivotal role in shaping the freedoms we now enjoy.

The Empress & The Prime Minister is built from ted's own words and actual speeches and debates from Pierre Trudeau's meteoric rise to political power, as well as selections from the arguments in the House of Commons as the issue of equality for Canada's Queer population was debated at the highest levels. These elements are mixed with imagined conversations, scenes from his life, and monologues that open a window on what it would have been like to be Queer in Canada in a much darker time. It's a Queer history, but it has impacted every Canadian.

The play opened in April 2019 at Theatre Network, and the run of the production coincided with the fiftieth anniversary of the passing of Bill C-150. During the run of the play, Alberta elected Jason Kenney as premier, who was definitely no ally to Canada's Queer population. At that same time, the Edmonton Police Service made a formal apology to the Queer community for decades of unfair scrutiny and abuse. A week later, thousands of students walked out of school to protest rollbacks in freedoms with regards to Gay–Straight Alliances. Some of them used the walkout to attend a student matinee of my play and were in tears during the Q&A that followed the show.

The past and the present were suddenly entwined. The ebb and flow of equality and rights became starkly clear that month. And even in my own community the debate raged about whether Bill C-150 actually improved our lives. The play became part of that conversation. Looking back, it's now clear that we were on the verge of a massive shift in politics, rights, and visions of our collective future.

When Mr. ted northe walked up the steps of Vancouver's courthouse in full drag in 1958, carrying a sign that said I AM A HUMAN BEING, he launched a defiant movement in Canadian history. For generations since, Queers and Queens and every other citizen of Canada have benefitted from his courage. These rights are for us all.

All plans to move forward with further productions were crushed by the pandemic (the second one in my lifetime). And in the broken world that emerged from that fracture, the art of drag suddenly became a lot more dangerous.

But in 2019, standing on that stage night after night sharing ted's story, I could sense that it was a narrative that people were craving. One human really can create change. The life of Mr. ted northe was proof.

The play was directed by Bradley Moss, and the versatile (and bilingual!) Joey Lespérance played Seattle's Rose Empress, Mama José, the Monsignor, Tommy Douglas, Robert Stanfield, Réal Caouette, and of course, Pierre Elliot Trudeau. *The Empress & The Prime Minister* was nominated for a Sterling Award for Outstanding New Play.

The world has shifted since I began exploring the phenomena of drag and using it as a platform for humour, politics, and Queer history. As the art of drag becomes a lightning rod for right-wing hate, homophobia, and transphobia, I am prouder every day that I stepped forward to share these stories. They cannot be untold now. These ideas, this joy cannot be contained.

This proud trio of Queens, both real and fictional, spans across my career, my imagination, and my duty. They have been steadfast companions as I evolve and mature. Every time I think they're buried in a distant past, they re-emerge in a new context and claim the stage again. They have voices that need to be heard now more than ever. The words they speak are funny and fierce, delightful and defiant.

This collection is dedicated to every young man who secretly dons his mother's jewels, daring to imagine a world beyond his own; and to every gender warrior who shares their personal transformation, changing the world around them.

Drag is more than a dress: it's armour against a cruel world. A declaration of being. An act of resistance.

WITH BELLS ON

For Neon

CHRISTOPHER PETERSON

Drag Artiste and Creator of Eyecons

IN 1985, when I was the reigning Empress of Vancouver, I travelled deep into the Prairies to pay homage to Lulu LaRude on her final night as Empress IX of Edmonton. For one of her many grand entrances of that evening, she entered as a bride, followed by three bridesmaids in a rainbow of pastel polyester from Value Village, complete with matching bouquets and cat-eye glasses. The final bridesmaid stood out — not only was she a foot taller than the others, but tucked into the bra of her bridesmaid gown was a Walkman. This Queen was already marching to her own music. That bridesmaid, bedecked in pastel yellow and pigtails, was Gloria Hole.

In the decade that followed, we lost track of each other. I moved to Toronto to build my one-man/many women show *Eyecons*, and Gloria transformed back into Darrin Hagen and began working as a theatre composer. Our paths crossed again in 1993 as we worked together on a stage musical adaptation of Craig Russell's film *Outrageous*. That was the same year that Darrin invited me to return annually to Edmonton for the now-famous Fringe Festival with his legendary drag troupe Guys In Disguise. And in 1996 as I performed my *Eyecons* show,

Darrin launched his career as playwright on a different Fringe stage with *The Edmonton Queen.*

In the ensuing decades, I saw Darrin evolve from drag queen to composer to writer to activist and now to documentary filmmaker. I moved to Key West to take up residency with my solo show, and Darrin stayed in Edmonton, honing his writing skills. It was in 2007 he told me I should come to Orlando to see the American debut of his play *BitchSlap!* at the Orlando Fringe. Two years later he was directing me in the role of Bette Davis at Key West's Waterfront Theatre, in a production that sold out before it opened and was remounted a year later. A few years later we teamed up to create *Typhoon Judy*, a musical delirium with Judy Garland on her near-death bed, which opened in Rehoboth Beach, Delaware, before being included in the Theatre Network season in Edmonton, and then the Waterfront Playhouse in Key West. Darrin and I share a fascination with diva celebrities, and the plays he crafted were perfectly honed for my impersonation skills.

It was 2009 when he told me about a drag Christmas comedy he was working on. I finally got around to watching the DVD while stuck in Key West with my husband during Hurricane Irma. In 2018, I directed *With Bells On* for its American premiere at the Red Barn Theatre in Key West. Once again I was struck by the insightful glimpse into the imagination and pain of a drag queen. When Darrin writes about that experience of transformation, it is with full empathy and authority. He has lived it, and so when his characters give voice to their inner fears or delusions of grandeur, or when they lash out with hubris or defiance, it's real. And even though no one in the theatre audience has ever run for Queen, you can feel them grabbing onto the hope, the exclusion, the feelings of doubt ... that impossible-to-describe experience is somehow shared with an audience who sees their own desires and hopes reflected in the life of an over-tall Glamazon dressed as a Christmas tree.

Every Queen wants a crown. In the pre-reality-TV drag-competition world, that crown was the only symbol of acceptance and triumph over a world that refused to make space for us. For many Queens it's the first time that our lifelong "liability" actually becomes an asset. My own time as Empress of Vancouver taught me what I was capable of. It was the stepping stone that led me towards decades of pursuing my dream of performing as a female impersonator.

When Darrin writes about drag queens, they aren't the joke. They're real people, courageous marginalized folk becoming activists to change the world, young men on the verge of awareness of the hypocrisy around them, and outsiders exploring gender fluidly, looking for a place where they finally fit in. He understands the power of transformation isn't just on the surface. It reaches profoundly deep into your soul. To see these words on the stage, spoken with authenticity, is a rare and thrilling experience.

PRODUCTION HISTORY

Lunchbox Theatre, Calgary, Alberta, 2010

Starring Paul Welch and Stafford Perry
Directed by Ian Prinsloo
Set and lighting design by Anton deGroot
Costume and makeup design by Norman J. McDonald
Sound design and choreography by Darrin Hagen
Stage management by Ailsa Birnie
2011 Betty Mitchell Award Nominee: Best New Play
2011 Betty Mitchell Award Winner: Paul Welch, Best Actor in a Comedy

Roxy Performance Series at Theatre Network, Edmonton, Alberta (produced by Guys In Disguise), 2011–2013

Starring Paul Welch and James Hamilton
Directed by Darrin Hagen
Set and lighting design by Paul Bezaire
Costume design by Norman J. McDonald
Sound design and choreography by Darrin Hagen
Makeup and stage management by Neon
2012 Elizabeth Sterling Haynes Award Nominee: Outstanding New Play
2012 Elizabeth Sterling Haynes Award Nominee: Outstanding Costume Design
2012 Elizabeth Sterling Haynes Award Nominee: Outstanding Independent Production

Ireland National One-Act Theatre Competition (multiple cities), 2013

Produced by Athlone Little Theatre
Starring Martin Kelleher and Declan Finn
Directed by Oliver Hegarty
2013 Letterkenny One-Act Festival Best Actor: Declan Finn
2013 Letterkenny One-Act Festival Best Play: Second Place
2013 Letterkenny One-Act Festival Adjudicator's Award: Best Costume

Lunchbox Theatre, Calgary, Alberta (co-produced by Guys In Disguise), 2014

Starring Paul Welch and Stafford Perry
Directed by Darrin Hagen
Set design by Paul Bezaire
Lighting design by Scott Peters
Costume design by Norman J. McDonald
Sound design and choreography by Darrin Hagen
Stage management by Sarah Minor
2015 Betty Mitchell Award Nominee: Stafford Perry, Best Actor in a Comedy
2015 Calgary Critics Award: Best Production of a Revival

New Vintage Theatre, Kelowna, British Columbia, 2016

Starring Shannon Lester (aka Sasha Zamolodchikova) and Zachary Richard Fox
Directed by Bonnie Gratz and Logan Mullin
Designed by Derek Gratz
Stage management by Bonnie Gratz

Red Barn Theatre, Key West, Florida, 2018

Starring Trey Gerrald and Don Bearden
Directed by Christopher Peterson
Set design by Gary McDonald and Jack McDonald
Lighting design by Jack McDonald
Costume and makeup design by Christopher Peterson
Choreography by Christopher Peterson
Stage management by Annie Miners

Varscona Theatre, Edmonton, Alberta (produced by Guys In Disguise), 2019

Starring Jake Tkaczyk and James Hamilton
Directed by Darrin Hagen
Set design by Paul Bezaire
Lighting design by Scott Peters
Costume design by Trevor Schmidt
Sound design and stage management by Darrin Hagen

Lunchbox Theatre, Calgary, Alberta, 2023

Starring Joel Schaefer and Bernardo Pacheco
Directed by Conrad Belau
Set design by Cassie Holmes
Lighting design by Lauren Acheson
Costume design by Benjamin Toner
Sound design by Darrin Hagen
Choreography by Alexa Elser
Fight direction by Haysam Kadri
Stage management by Meredith Johnson

Richmond Triangle Players, Richmond, Virginia, 2024

Starring Luke Newsome (aka Wette Midler) and Doug Schneider
Directed by Joe Pabst
Set design by William Luther
Lighting design by Gabe Beard
Costume design by Alex Valentin
Stage management by Lucian Restivo

PRODUCTION NOTES

THE ELEVATOR "DINGS" indicated in the script are thirty seconds apart on the elevator ride down.

THE ELEVATOR "DINGS" are twenty seconds apart on the elevator ride up.

THE LONG AWKWARD PAUSES are part of the rhythm. Embrace them.

Image courtesy of Ian Jackson / EPIC Photography; used with permission

Image courtesy of Ian Jackson / EPIC Photography; used with permission

He stands in the hallway, waiting for the elevator. It arrives with a ***ding!*** *He steps onto the elevator. He presses the ground button, and the door starts to close.*

"SHE": Wait! Wait!

He hits the "door open" button. He waits. His face changes as "She" moves closer.

"She" is at least six feet tall, wearing staggeringly high heels and heavy glitzy makeup. Her outfit is a combination of showgirl and Christmas tree. The skirt is a giant silver hoop festooned with Christmas decorations, including bells that jingle loudly as she approaches. The headdress is a giant star with silver rays shooting out in all directions. She stops in the hallway and sprays some perfume on herself. She tilts and turns to manipulate the epic costume into the elevator.

"SHE": Much appreciated.

HE: Of course.

Pause.

"SHE": I hate waiting for the elevators in this building. Sometimes you wait for hours.

HE: Yes. Yes, you do.

He is frozen, staring at her.

"SHE": Ground floor, please.

HE: Yes, I know.

Pause. She looks at him expectantly. They wait. Uncomfortable silence.

"SHE": You need to take your finger off the button.

HE: Pardon?

"SHE": The button. We're not moving.

HE: Oh! (*He laughs nervously.*) There we go!

The elevator door slowly closes and the elevator starts roughly descending the building.

Pause. He sniffs the air. ***DING!***

HE: That perfume.

"SHE": Hm?

HE: Your perfume.

"SHE": What about it?

HE: It's — intoxicating.

"SHE": Well, then, don't drink it.

Long pause. ***DING!***

HE: Amazing view, isn't it?

"SHE": What?

HE: Your view. Do you like it?

"SHE": Yes.

HE: Same here.

"SHE": Pardon?

HE: I live on the fourteenth floor as well. Fourteen oh seven.

"SHE": Sigh.

HE: You — don't recognize me?

"SHE": I've never seen you in the elevator before.

HE: I've been using the stairs a lot.

"SHE": Ahh.

HE: Good for the —

"SHE": Yes?

HE: Lungs.

"SHE": Right.

Pause. ***DING!***

HE: Long ride.

She gives him a withering glance.

HE: The elevator.

"SHE": It always is.

HE: Your — hat is really —

"SHE": It's a headdress.

HE: Big. Right.

"SHE": And it's the perfect size.

HE: It's very —

"SHE": It's just —

HE: — shiny.

"SHE": — tinsel and stuff.

HE: It's pretty.

"SHE": Thank you.

HE: You're welcome. Are those —?

"SHE": Christmas balls.

Pause. ***DING!***

HE: Do you enjoy living on the fourteenth floor?

"SHE": Thirteenth.

HE: Excuse me?

"SHE": They skip a floor when they're numbering. We live on the thirteenth floor.

HE: I — never thought of it that way.

"SHE": Not that it matters. All the floors are the same.

HE: Huh.

"SHE": You're not superstitious, are you?

HE: No. But now that you mention it — the thirteenth floor hasn't been very good for me.

Pause. ***DING!***

HE: Do you — dress like this very often?

"SHE": Like what?

HE: This — head thing and all the — sparkly stuff.

"SHE": Only for special occasions.

HE: Of course. (*pause*) Like?

"SHE": Excuse me?

HE: Special occasions like —?

"SHE": Like tonight.

HE: Okay. You don't wanna talk about it.

"SHE": Well, we don't really know each other —

HE: Of course —

"SHE": I mean, I'm a pretty private person.

HE: Yes. Yes, you are.

"SHE": I mean, until today, I hadn't even laid eyes on you —

HE: But I noticed you when I first moved in.

"SHE": Of course you did.

HE: I can smell your perfume after you've been on the elevator.

"SHE": I'll try to wear less.

HE: No, don't. It's nice.

"SHE": Thank you.

Pause. ***DING!***

HE: Your window kinda faces mine.

"SHE": What?

HE: My view — is of you.

Pause.

"SHE": Okay, you're not one of those Peeping Toms, are you?

HE: NO! God no!

"SHE": Because I know the guy that runs the management company —

HE: You do?

"SHE": Yes, I do.

HE: That's great!

"SHE": You won't think it's so great when I tell him that one of my neighbours is spying on me.

HE: NO! You can tell him about the elevator!

The elevator suddenly clunks roughly to a stop. She gives a look that could kill.

"SHE": What about the elevator?

HE: It's always getting stuck.

"SHE": Great.

HE: Great.

"SHE": I don't have time for this.

She hits the emergency call button. A loud bell rings.

HE: That — won't really do much.

"SHE": What?

HE: It just rings in the hallway.

"SHE": Well, what good does that do?

HE: None really. Unless someone comes out to see why it's ringing.

"SHE": Great. Do you have a phone?

HE: Yes, but —

"SHE": Hand it over.

HE: Okay, but —

He digs for his phone. She rings the emergency bell again and again.

"SHE": HELP! Isn't this the floor where —

BOTH: — all the old folks live?

"SHE": Great. Just great. None of them will hear the bell.

HE: Here's my cell, but —

"SHE": Perfect!

She opens it and tries getting a signal.

HE: It's kinda like a bunker in here —

"SHE": How come it's not working?

HE: Almost impossible to get a signal.

"SHE": Does this phone work?

HE: Yes, usually.

"SHE": Great. Your phone's not working.

She tosses it without looking. It hits the floor. She rings the bell again, obnoxiously.

"SHE": I don't get it. The elevator always works for me.

HE: I think it's my fault.

"SHE": What?

HE: I have really bad luck with this elevator.

"SHE": You should've told me that before I got on.

HE: I held it for you. I was being neighbourly —

"SHE": Neighbours don't peek in neighbours' windows.

HE: I don't —

"SHE": Neighbours —

HE: — peek —

"SHE": — mind their own business.

HE: I — keep to myself.

"SHE": Yeah. Except for the spying.

He sits on the floor and relaxes.

"SHE": What is this? Start doing something.

HE: This *is* what to do. Wait for someone to report it.

"SHE": You're just going to sit there?

HE: Not a good idea to waste your energy.

"SHE": As you can tell from my ensemble, I have plans for later.

HE: I've been through this before.

"SHE": I haven't! *(She rings the bell some more, obnoxiously)* HELP! HEEEEEEELLLLPP!

HE: You have to calm down.

"SHE": You have to learn to fight back.

HE: Sometimes you need to accept —

"SHE": Stop trying to get the last word!

HE: What's the big deal? It's just a matter of time.

She leans against the wall. It's starting to sink in.

"SHE": You don't understand. Time is the one thing I don't have.

Pause. Finally, he stands. He holds out a hand.

HE: I'm Ted.

She doesn't shake his hand, just stares at him.

"SHE": Hello, Teddy.

TED: Ted — it's not — I prefer Ted.

"SHE": Okay. Ted.

TED: And your name is —

"SHE": — not important.

TED: What?

"SHE": Look, no offence, Teddy —

TED: Ted.

"SHE": Whatever. Until I find out that you're not some kinda weirdo, my name is my business.

TED: I understand.

"SHE": Just stay in your corner and no funny stuff.

TED: Really, I'm not like that. You have the wrong impression.

"SHE": We'll see.

Pause.

TED: This is the kind of luck I have.

"SHE": What?

TED: I finally head out — for an adventure — and I mess it up.

"SHE": You gotta get out more.

TED: It was my New Year's resolution.

"SHE": Getting out?

TED: Yes.

"SHE": And have you? Gotten out?

TED: I was going to start tonight.

"SHE": It's almost Christmas.

TED: I like to visualize before I act.

She rolls her eyes. Long pause.

"SHE": Where were you gonna go?

TED: I was just going to walk around. Check things out.

"SHE": Like — to a club?

TED: I don't think so. Something nice. Quiet.

"SHE": You can stay home and get that.

TED: Baby steps.

"SHE": I guess.

Pause.

"SHE": Alone?

TED: Pardon?

"SHE": Were you going to go out alone?

TED: I *was* hoping to run into someone. (*pause*) I wanted to see where — someone like you went on a night like this.

"SHE": So you *are* stalking me!

TED: No!

"SHE": I knew it!

TED: Please —

"SHE": I know martial arts, buddy.

TED: You won't —

"SHE": I have my fuchsia belt in whipping your butt.

TED: I'm really normal —

"SHE": Yeah, right.

TED: Too normal. Don't be scared of me.

"SHE": I'm not scared of you.

TED: Good.

"SHE": Not even a little bit.

TED: That's good. That's very good.

Pause.

"SHE": If anyone should be scared, it should be you.

TED: I am.

"SHE": You should be.

TED: A little.

"SHE": Good.

Pause. She dekes him; he flinches.

"SHE": Have you ever tried prying the doors open?

TED: I'm not strong enough. Plus, we're dangling seven floors up. I wouldn't want to mess with that.

"SHE": So we just — wait?

TED: Yup. Have a seat.

"SHE": Does it look like I can sit down?

TED: Sorry.

Long pause.

"SHE": I suppose you're wondering why I'm dressed like this.

TED: No.

"SHE": Really?

TED: I assume you work at some — magical crystal palace.

"SHE": Close enough.

TED: Some place full of really — interesting people.

"SHE": You got that right.

TED: Folks who know how to have fun.

"SHE": To say the least.

TED: Must be nice.

"SHE": Must be.

TED: I bet.

Pause.

TED: Are you — a showgirl?

"SHE": No, I park cars at the club.

TED: Oh.

"SHE": Of course I'm a showgirl.

TED: Oh!

"SHE": But if I don't get there by midnight, I'm just a girl. No show.

TED: Just a girl?

"SHE": Just a girl.

TED: You could never be just a girl.

"SHE": What's that supposed to mean?

TED: Look at you. You're — you're —

"SHE": I don't like where this is going.

TED: No — it's a good thing. To stand out the way you do.

"SHE": Yeah?

TED: I wish — I wish I could do that.

"SHE": Anyone can do that.

TED: I couldn't.

"SHE": Sure you could.

TED: Not like — that.

"SHE": Well, no, not like this.

TED: I'm better in the background.

"SHE": Is that what you were going to do tonight? Lurk around in the background?

TED: I wouldn't have lurked.

"SHE": Well, if you're not standing out, you're lurking.

TED: Someone has to stay in the background and watch.

"SHE": And why is that?

TED: Not everyone can be the show. Some of us need to be the audience.

Pause.

"SHE": Natasha.

TED: Pardon?

NATASHA: I'm Natasha.

TED: Oh. Oh! Very nice meeting you, Natasha.

NATASHA: Of course it is.

Pause.

TED: When — when I first moved in, I thought you had a roommate.

NATASHA: Oh really?

TED: Yes. I watched you come home —

NATASHA: Your view doesn't include my changing room, does it?

TED: Your what? No!

NATASHA: Continue.

TED: You have a change room?

NATASHA: It's — really more like a large closet. But I prefer not to use that word.

TED: Wow, my place really sucks.

NATASHA: Your story?

TED: I said to myself, "There's a gal who has a real interesting life."

NATASHA: Talking to yourself?

TED: And then, the next day — I saw her.

NATASHA: Her?

TED: The red head.

NATASHA: You mean —

TED: I couldn't believe how beautiful.

NATASHA: But —

TED: She moved with such assurance, such grace —

NATASHA: It's all in the shoes.

TED: I wanted to meet her so bad — She was so different. A quiet, dignified beauty.

NATASHA: Dignified, huh?

TED: She always stood so tall and straight.

NATASHA: Posture is important.

TED: After she got on the elevator, I would step into the hallway. All that would be left behind was a trace of perfume. I would breathe it in and wish ...

NATASHA: Yes?

TED: ...

NATASHA: What would you wish?

TED: Of course, eventually I realized — there was no red-headed girl. One night I actually saw you put the wig on just as you stepped out of your entrance.

NATASHA: My secret identity: Revealed!

TED: Yeah, I know ... it seems silly now that I know.

NATASHA: Welcome to the real world, Teddy.

TED: Thanks. I think. You were very convincing as — her.

NATASHA: A girl's gotta be versatile.

TED: I do have one question though —

NATASHA: What's that?

TED: Who's the guy?

Pause.

NATASHA: The guy?

TED: The guy.

NATASHA: You're kidding, right?

TED: Is he a — boyfriend? Is that the word you people use now?

NATASHA: Oh my god.

TED: Does he work in construction or something?

NATASHA: Yes, he does.

TED: I never would have guessed.

NATASHA: Guessed what?

TED: That he was —

NATASHA: That he was — what?

TED: He's pretty — masculine.

NATASHA: *(in her lowest, most macho voice)* Thanks.

A long pause as he puts it together. He looks at her closely.

TED: Really?

NATASHA: Dressing like this takes balls.

TED: Wow. I never would have —

NATASHA: That's the whole point.

TED: How could I have missed that?

NATASHA: I am a Mistress of Illusion.

TED: How did I not see that? Do I really go through life oblivious to the obvious?

NATASHA: Ummm ... this is not a great time for an existential crisis.

TED: That's why I'm alone, isn't it?

NATASHA: There's probably a million other reasons —

TED: Oh great!

NATASHA: That came out wrong.

TED: Why would you say that?

NATASHA: I was trying to be supportive.

TED: That wasn't supportive!

NATASHA: I see that now. It's a problem I have.

TED: Not being supportive?

NATASHA: Talking without thinking. That's why *I'm* alone.

Pause.

NATASHA: This is NOT how I wanted to spend my Saturday night.

TED: We'll get out in time for your — engagement.

NATASHA: I don't want to get my hopes up.

TED: Yeah. I know what you mean. I don't think I want to go out anymore.

NATASHA: What? Oh, c'mon, Teddy. You can't just give up like that.

TED: Apparently, it's what I do best.

Pause.

NATASHA: So what can you see? When you look into my place?

TED: Just your front entrance.

NATASHA: I don't want you looking anymore.

TED: That's my only window.

NATASHA: Wow. Your place really does suck.

TED: I'm in transition —

NATASHA: Transition from what to what?

TED: From — happy and not alone to — alone.

NATASHA: Hey, I'm sorry.

Long pause.

TED: I'm going to really let the building manager have it when we get out of here.

NATASHA: It's not his fault.

TED: I hate this building.

NATASHA: There's way worse places.

TED: I should've kept my loft.

NATASHA: You have a loft?

TED: Had. I just sold it.

NATASHA: You sold a loft and moved into a crap apartment with one window?

TED: Yeah.

NATASHA: Why?

TED: I couldn't go back. I don't want to talk about it.

NATASHA: Fine. Fine.

He turns away and pouts. She finds some candy canes in her bag and offers him one. He ignores her. She pulls an iPod out of her purse. Then she puts her headphones on.

TED: What are you doing?

She ignores him, immersed in her music.

TED: What are you listening to?

She ignores him.

TED: Is that the music they play at the magical —

NATASHA: What?

TED: I was just wondering about the music —

NATASHA: I thought you didn't want to talk.

TED: Well, no, actually I just didn't want to talk about —

NATASHA: So this is me not talking.

TED: The loft — I didn't want to talk about that.

Pause.

NATASHA: It's my number.

TED: What?

NATASHA: For tonight.

TED: You mean your showgirl song?

NATASHA: If I ever get out, that is.

TED: We'll get out.

NATASHA: Just for the record, if we don't get out, I'll never forgive you.

TED: We'll get out.

She sways to the music and then starts lip-synching and doing the moves.

TED: What are you doing? Oh, I see. You're practising, aren't you? Hello? Is — is that your showgirl performance? Hello?

He taps her shoulder, scaring her. She takes off her headphones.

NATASHA: WHAT????

TED: I was just — is that — that's your performance, isn't it?

NATASHA: No, it's the drag queen workout.

TED: Really?

NATASHA: Okay, rule number one: my first answer is always sarcastic.

TED: Oh.

NATASHA: Some people think it's funny when I do that.

He manages a weak laugh.

NATASHA: Okay, I don't need your pity party.

TED: It's like you speak a whole different version of English.

NATASHA: Yes. The Queen's English.

TED: Really? But — Oh! I get it.

NATASHA: Can you let me do my work, please?

TED: I'd like to see that.

NATASHA: You're about to.

TED: Can you turn the music up?

NATASHA: It's an iPod, not a boombox.

TED: Of course.

NATASHA: The only way to hear it is with the headphones.

TED: Okay. I'll just watch then.

She performs a routine for a bit. We hear nothing but the tinny strains of disco through her headphones. He sits and watches politely, not really comprehending. Finally she stops on a grand ending gesture. She waits for his applause. None comes.

NATASHA: Well?

TED: What?

NATASHA: What do you think?

TED: I didn't really understand what you were doing.

NATASHA: But would you vote for me?

TED: What's your platform?

NATASHA: Six inches of clear Plexi.

TED: What??

NATASHA: With jewelled straps. Keep with the tour, Teddy.

TED: I'm probably not the person to ask —

NATASHA: Who else am I gonna ask?

TED: I mean, I have no context for what you're doing —

NATASHA: I need an informed opinion. Come here.

He stands. She takes one earplug and puts it in his ear.

NATASHA: Now you'll be able to hear. But the cord is short. So stick right beside me. Do what I do.

The music starts: a lively disco or drag Christmas song. Suddenly, he is in her world of sparkle and applause. She starts lip-synching. He watches her, fascinated, tentatively bopping along with her. She does a big move to the side, and he follows so his earpiece doesn't fall out. She gestures grandly with her arm — he echoes the move.

He gains confidence.He performs the moves with gusto. As they get to the musical bridge, she screams.

NATASHA: Kickline!

TED: What?

NATASHA: Kickline! Get ready!

The music heads into the big finish. They lock arms and begin the kickline. But the combined weight of their bouncing isn't good for the elevator. There is a loud CLUNK and they wipe out as the elevator plummets and then slams to a halt. The lights flicker and flash and then go out with a sizzle. Total darkness.

TED: This is not good!

NATASHA: Oh my god!

TED: Are you okay?

NATASHA: NO!

TED: What's wrong? What's broken?

NATASHA: My iPod!

TED: That's it?

NATASHA: That's enough!

TED: We're trapped in a box with limited oxygen and no light and you're worried about your iPod??

NATASHA: Relax, Teddy Bear. If you stop freaking out, there will be enough air.

TED: I'm not freaking out!

NATASHA: Where I come from, we call that freaking out.

TED: This is not good.

NATASHA: Just breathe. I'm right here.

TED: I don't like the dark.

NATASHA: Well, no wonder you never go out at night.

TED: In the dark — it feels smaller in here. I can't take it. The walls are closing in —

NATASHA: You're imagining things.

TED: No — no, I can feel them —

NATASHA: It's an illusion.

TED: Light! I need light!

NATASHA: Oh, Jesus Christ!

TED: Let there be light!

She flicks a switch on her outfit. The entire headpiece lights up, Christmas-style. They are posed as "The Pietà," with him in her lap.

TED: Wow. You're like an angel!

NATASHA: Just pray that the batteries last until showtime.

As if in answer to her prayer, the backup generator turns the emergency lights on. His panic ebbs.

TED: Don't worry, you'll get there by midnight. Someone's going to come into the building. Someone's going to need to use the elevator. When they see that it's stuck, they'll call the fire department.

NATASHA: Great. I finally get a chance to make an impression on some firefighters and I'm dressed like a Christmas tree. This is the story of my life. Always the wrong outfit for the occasion. I should've known I couldn't pull this off. I'm the Queen who wears paisley when everyone else is wearing plaid. I never think things through.

TED: What's wrong with this? You look fine.

NATASHA: "Fine"? Hello!!! I have a halo! My head is lit up! I'm twinkling my cotton gusset off over here — and all you can say is "fine"? Not "amazing"? Not "fabulous"?

TED: Well, sure, I guess.

NATASHA: Great. There goes my big finish.

TED: What?

NATASHA: This special effect was gonna win me the pageant.

TED: No, really — it's pretty neat —

NATASHA: I would also have accepted "stunning" —

TED: Okay — "fabulous" —

NATASHA: No. If you meant that you would have said that.

TED: I would have? No — it's just that those aren't words I use very much.

NATASHA: Why not?

TED: I prefer a more measured response to things.

NATASHA: I see. Let me know how that works out for you.

TED: It works fine.

NATASHA: Right. That's why you're heading out on a weekend for the first time ever.

TED: Do you have to rub it in?

Pause.

NATASHA: How long does it usually take to get rescued?

TED: That depends. I was in here for four hours once.

NATASHA: Great.

TED: I'll do my best to keep us entertained.

NATASHA: In four hours my beard will be showing.

TED: Beard?

NATASHA: I hope there are no photographers.

TED: You can grow a beard in four hours?

NATASHA: Or eligible bachelors on the rescue team.

TED: This moustache took me two years.

NATASHA: This is gonna get awkward.

TED: It doesn't have to —

NATASHA: I'm going to have to go to the bathroom eventually.

TED: I won't watch.

NATASHA: It's not that. It's — kind of a two-person job.

TED: What? WHAT?? NO!

NATASHA: I can hold it.

TED: Good. Because *I'm* not gonna!

NATASHA: Change the subject.

TED: Okay. Where do you work?

NATASHA: I'm a showgirl. I work at the Magical Crystal Palace.

TED: Please don't make fun of me.

NATASHA: I'm not. That's actually the name.

TED: Do you enjoy being a showgirl?

NATASHA: To say the least. Although —

TED: Yes?

NATASHA: One wearies of being stared at like a freak.

TED: They don't.

NATASHA: Can I tell you a story?

TED: Is it going to scare me?

NATASHA: I doubt it. There was one day — I was bringing all of my stuff home from a show — and it's a lot of stuff. So I'm getting out of the taxi, and it's a total production. I have two wig heads — not the stubby ones, but the ones with the long necks — with big pink-and-silver up-dos, bubble-curls everywhere, three feather boas, which I throw around my neck, and a small accordion covered in beads and dangly bits, plus a harp —

TED: A harp?

NATASHA: It goes with the mermaid tail.

TED: Mermaid tail?

NATASHA: My story?

TED: Go ahead.

NATASHA: A mermaid tail, which you have to carry with the fins up, otherwise the sequined seaweed will drag on the dirty —

TED: Sequined seaweed?

NATASHA: Well, yes. It goes with the pearl clamshells.

TED: I'm afraid to ask.

NATASHA: For my bosom. *(pause)* They're big clams.

TED: Of course.

NATASHA: Okay, so I'm standing beside the taxi, looking for money — but with all this stuff draped all over me, I must look like Liberace's clothesline.

And all of a sudden, this pickup truck comes around the corner — fast, squealing out — heads straight towards me. And then, not one but TWO cop cars, sirens and lights full blast. It's a high-speed chase. And they're gonna drive right by me.

The pickup truck is coming towards me fast. It's this redneck dude, totally freaked out, and beside him his girlfriend. She looks like all the girls I went to high school with — you know, tight t-shirt, long hair, curling-iron-no-brush — you know?

TED: I do know.

NATASHA: And they're like Butch and Sundance. Or Thelma and Louise. No! They're a modern redneck, white-trash Bonnie and Clyde. And the girl is holding on for dear life as they careen down the street. The cops are right behind them. And that's when it happens.

TED: What happens?

NATASHA: They look straight at me. And it's like — we're all frozen for a second. And I can see right through the windshield and into their lives. And our worlds come together. In a movie, it would all go slow-motion right then. And it kinda did. My feather boas were blowing in the breeze, and a big piece of pink chiffon fell out of my grip and unfurled. And the look on their face — shock? Surprise? Or was it just "What the fu —?"

And they sailed past me in this — this scene from a movie — tires screeching, through the intersection, rush-hour traffic stopped in every direction. And then the cops drove past — and gave me the same look!

And then they were gone. And I was standing on my street, still holding all my stuff, and I looked over my shoulder at where the chase had disappeared ...

And that's when I noticed.

TED: Noticed what?

NATASHA: There were a dozen cars stopped. And every one of the drivers, and all of their passengers — were all staring at me.

TED: Is that unusual?

NATASHA: A high-speed chase had just barged through their lives! But they were staring at the drag queen with the giant mermaid tail sticking up in the air.

TED: Surely you can understand —

NATASHA: Where are people's priorities?

TED: I mean, it's not every day —

NATASHA: What did you feel when I walked on this elevator?

TED: Feel?

NATASHA: Don't think. Just answer.

TED: I don't — nothing.

NATASHA: You weren't scared?

TED: No. A little. Yes.

NATASHA: But why?

TED: Well — I don't know how to say this, but — you're gigantic.

NATASHA: But I'm harmless!

TED: The rest of the world doesn't know that.

NATASHA: What's wrong with being a huge drag queen??

TED: Nothing. It's just that — well, not everyone *is*.

NATASHA: I suppose.

TED: And if you choose this life —

NATASHA: Are you saying I chose this?

TED: No, that's — I mean —

NATASHA: Because the only choice I had was whether to make this outfit in gold or silver!

TED: Of course.

NATASHA: And how much leg to show!

TED: Right.

NATASHA: And whether or not to shave my —!

She breaks down, overwhelmed by the shaving sacrifice. She fans her lashes.

TED: Hey.

NATASHA: What now?

TED: Thanks. For the story.

NATASHA: Whatever.

TED: No, I learned something.

NATASHA: What?

TED: You're pretty brave.

NATASHA: Yeah?

TED: And you shouldn't be upset when people stare.

NATASHA: Why not?

TED: Because when people see something special, or rare, they stare.

NATASHA: They stare at train wrecks too.

TED: True.

NATASHA: You're no help.

TED: You're an event. In their lives. People go through life doing the same thing over and over, living the same day again and again. It's what we do. And every now and then, there's an event. Something that shocks you, or surprises you — doesn't matter, it's an event that reminds you that life can still be interesting. It can always throw something at you that — well, in a zillion years you would never expect it.

And it becomes a currency, something that sets you apart. And for a few days, you're the guy that got stuck in the elevator with a drag queen. And everyone asks you about it. And you can laugh. And be the centre of attention. Those people who saw you — they're going to talk about that for a long time.

Long awkward pause.

NATASHA: I'm sure this will be a great story for the guys at work.

TED: I won't tell.

NATASHA: How come? If I were you and I was stuck here with someone dressed like me, I would want to tell someone.

TED: I don't know —

NATASHA: I think this would definitely count as an event.

TED: Definitely. But — I don't really have anyone to tell it to.

NATASHA: Really? What's the matter with you?

TED: I'm — still rebuilding. From the divorce.

NATASHA: You need to move on.

TED: I know. But — it's so much harder than I thought it would be. My friends — our friends, I mean — were actually *her* friends.

NATASHA: Tell you what. You have my express permission to use this story as currency. At work. With *your* friends.

TED: Really?

NATASHA: Absolutely.

TED: That's fabulous.

NATASHA: Did you just say "fabulous"?

TED: I guess I did.

NATASHA: Finally! Some progress!

TED: I need some new friends, though.

NATASHA: I know what you mean. I need new backup dancers.

TED: That's — not really the same —

She picks up her iPod.

NATASHA: How am I gonna practise now?

TED: Here. Give it to me.

NATASHA: No! Well — okay.

She hands it to him. He touches one thing, and it starts working.

TED: There.

NATASHA: What did you do?

TED: You had the safety lock on.

NATASHA: Oh. Thanks.

TED: No more kicklines, okay?

NATASHA: I guess I could pull it back a bit. Too bad — you were pretty good at it.

TED: Really?

NATASHA: Yeah. Most straight guys —

TED: What?

NATASHA: I mean — I'm sorry, I didn't mean to assume —

TED: No — it's okay.

NATASHA: Are you?

TED: Am I what?

NATASHA: You know what? It doesn't matter.

TED: It doesn't?

NATASHA: No.

Pause.

TED: So why Christmas?

NATASHA: Pardon?

TED: Christmas. I mean, no offence, but it seems like — I don't know — there might be a more appropriate night for a guy — girl like you —

NATASHA: More appropriate? Like what?

TED: I don't know — something a little less — holy.

NATASHA: It's not my fault that Christians grabbed all the good long weekends. What have you got in mind? Arbour Day? Labour Day?

TED: How about Halloween?

NATASHA: Too obvious. Do you know what drag queens call Halloween?

TED: What?

NATASHA: Amateur Night. Every frat boy from here to eternity wants to do drag on Halloween. Big fucking deal. Try doing it on a Tuesday and then we'll talk. Besides, Christmas is the gayest holiday of all. "Don we now our gay apparel." "Fall on your knees." "Santa Clause is coming.". "Ding dong merrily on high." "Come, they told me, par-rum-pum-pum-pum." Need I say more?

TED: Wow. You make everything sound gay.

NATASHA: It's a gift.

TED: I would love to see your show sometime.

NATASHA: Yeah?

TED: I felt like I was actually in your world for a second.

NATASHA: You did?

TED: Absolutely. I could even hear the applause.

NATASHA: It was a live recording. That way if nobody claps, I'll still hear applause.

TED: Ah.

NATASHA: But you certainly have a good sense of rhythm.

TED: I do?

NATASHA: You do.

TED: My ex-wife always told me I couldn't dance to save my life.

NATASHA: She sounds like my ex-wife.

Pause.

TED: I'm sorry — did you say —?

NATASHA: What?

TED: Ex —?

NATASHA: Yes.

TED: Wow.

NATASHA: What?

TED: Just — wow.

NATASHA: It's not like I was just born in this outfit.

TED: Of course.

NATASHA: I mean, I had a life before this.

TED: I should have realized —

NATASHA: One does not just arrive fully formed.

TED: That's a good piece of advice —

NATASHA: One needs to blossom — unfurl, if you will —

TED: Did she — know?

NATASHA: About?

TED: All of this?

NATASHA: "This" had nothing to do with it.

TED: What happened?

NATASHA: You ask a lot of questions, Teddy Bear.

TED: I'm interested.

NATASHA: Yeah?

TED: You're my first Queen.

NATASHA: That you know of.

TED: What?

NATASHA: Trust me. We are everywhere. (*pause*) So now it's my turn to be nosy. Why?

TED: Why?

NATASHA: Why did you end up alone in this building?

TED: We wanted different things. She needed to grow.

NATASHA: And you?

TED: I needed — I don't know. It didn't seem to be about what I needed.

NATASHA: I'm sorry.

TED: But — chin up, eh, my man? (*He punches her chin, buddy-style. She freezes.*) Oh — I'm sorry —

NATASHA: Relax.

She checks her compact for damage, then relaxes.

TED: You move very well for such a —

NATASHA: Watch it —

TED: — statuesque performer.

NATASHA: (*pleased*) "Statuesque"?

TED: I'm trying.

NATASHA: I like it! Those were some pretty mean moves you were tossing around.

TED: Nah.

NATASHA: No, really! You have a bit of flourish in you.

TED: Actually, I'm Danish.

NATASHA: What? Ahh! Not bad. For an amateur.

TED: I love to dance.

NATASHA: Why don't you dance more?

TED: She thought my dancing was — too flourish-y.

NATASHA: I wasn't aware there was such a thing.

TED: And so I stopped.

NATASHA: Well, I think that's about to change.

TED: What?

NATASHA: You're coming out with me tonight.

TED: What?

NATASHA: We're going dancing!

She stands and shimmies the outfit to full effect.

TED: No, I couldn't!

NATASHA: With those moves? Yes, you could.

TED: To the — Sparkly Castle?

NATASHA: Close enough.

TED: I don't think they'll let me in.

NATASHA: Darling, if you're with me, they'll let you in.

TED: Really?

NATASHA: Bouncers don't argue with someone dressed like this.

TED: Godzilla wouldn't argue with someone dressed like that.

NATASHA: There is the odd advantage to being odd.

TED: But we're going to have to get out first.

NATASHA: You need one of those bursts of adrenaline — like when the grandma lifts the car off the baby.

TED: I'm afraid if it hasn't happened by now, it won't —

NATASHA: See, your problem is you give up too easy.

TED: Yes, you're right, I do —

NATASHA: There! You did it again!

TED: What?

NATASHA: You just agreed with me.

TED: But — I mean, I didn't — I don't know what I should say.

NATASHA: Tell me to mind my own business.

TED: Okay. Mind your own business.

NATASHA: Fat chance. Okay, Teddy, here's the plan. I'll lift you up and you can remove the fan thingy and then crawl through the little hole thingy, into the shaft thingy, and pry the elevator doors open.

TED: I don't think so.

NATASHA: C'mon! I really have to get out of here.

TED: You do it then.

NATASHA: I can't fit through that hole.

TED: I'll get stuck.

NATASHA: Please, Teddy Bear? I've been working towards this night for months.

TED: What happens tonight?

Pause.

NATASHA: You'll laugh.

TED: Tell me.

NATASHA: Tonight's the night I become the Queen.

TED: Looks like you already are —

NATASHA: Not *a* Queen. *The* Queen. The Christmas Queen.

TED: Of the —

NATASHA: Magical Crystal Palace.

TED: Tonight?

NATASHA: Tonight.

TED: Surely they will wait until you get there to give it to you.

NATASHA: It doesn't get given. It has to be won.

TED: Oh.

NATASHA: And if I don't show up, they'll assume I chickened out.

TED: There's always next Christmas.

NATASHA: No. It has to be now.

TED: Why now?

NATASHA: If I don't do it now, I never will.

TED: I know exactly what you mean.

NATASHA: Girls like me — well, let's just say there's a shelf life. A best-before date.

TED: I feel like time is running out too.

NATASHA: Yeah, right.

TED: I'm at a crossroads.

NATASHA: Is that what you call it?

TED: Do I turn, or do I go straight?

NATASHA: Pardon?

TED: Wait — I didn't mean —

NATASHA: Then don't say straight. Say "gaily forward."

TED: I can't say that.

NATASHA: Too soon?

TED: Maybe just a bit. Are you at a crossroads?

NATASHA: I need to prove something to myself.

TED: That you're the Christmas Queen of the Magical Crystal Palace?

NATASHA: I guess expensive lofts and fancy cars are the real way to change your life.

TED: That's not fair.

NATASHA: I knew you wouldn't get it.

TED: I just don't know how this will make your life better.

NATASHA: Let's just say my professional showgirl career got off to a bumpy start. And if I can get there tonight I might be able to fix it. I just gotta show those bitches I can rise above it.

TED: I thought they were your friends.

NATASHA: So did I.

Pause.

NATASHA: My very first professional gig was last summer. It was a great idea on paper. I was hired to entertain at a street performer festival.

TED: Like — a clown?

NATASHA: Sort of. But with way better hair. And makeup. And bigger shoes. And I told all the girls at the Magical Crystal Palace that I had booked my first real gig. And they laughed at me.

TED: They did?

NATASHA: They did. But I said to them, "Just wait. My picture will be in the paper. I'm gonna be a star and leave all this behind."

TED: So ... how did the gig go?

NATASHA: Let's just say only a few kids cried.

TED: Kids?

NATASHA: I'm about to reveal a very painful memory that has scarred me ever since.

TED: You said it was last summer —

NATASHA: Please don't interrupt me when I'm exaggerating. Anyway, I figured in this day and age, drag queens are kinda everywhere, so I wanted to do something the kids would love — not just drag, but something just for them. And so I had this mermaid tail made.

TED: The one you hold up so the sequins don't drag.

NATASHA: Now this tail — once it's on, you can't really walk. Because it's a giant fin, right?

TED: Of ... course?

NATASHA: Kids love mermaids. What could go wrong?

So I have to find a place to — pose. So I think, I'll get way up high — on top of something. Lucky for me, there's a trailer in the middle of the park being used as a ticket booth. So I arrange for the staff to meet me at the ticket booth with a big ladder. I climb up and sit on the edge of the roof and pull on the tail.

TED: What's under the tail?

NATASHA: Wouldn't you like to know?

TED: No. I wouldn't.

NATASHA: A Speedo. That's all I can really wear under it. Anyway, from my perch, I can see the whole park. Now, my plan is to basically pose for photos and say hello.

But I kinda miscalculated. First of all, it's July. And it's noon. And I'm on a hot tin roof. Within five minutes I start to fry on one cheek ... like a well-done fish stick.

Below me, I see a little boy. So I wave. He waves back. I flap my tail. His eyes light up. Finally! I'm having an impact. Bringing joy to a tiny corner of the world!

He calls out "Hi, little mermaid!" I call back: "Hey kid! How's it going?" And his jaw drops. And he drops his ice cream cone. Even at the best of times, I sound like a trucker.

He starts peppering me with questions. Hard questions. "How did you get way up there? Can you fly?" I explain that I have fairy wings. "No, you don't. Mermaids don't have wings." I think he knows the Rules of Mermaids better than I do.

"How come your voice is so low?" I explain that it's a modern era and that gender is fluid.

A group of businessmen strolls by. I strike a pose, arm high in the air — but by doing that, my clamshell bra slips, and my nipple is revealed.

The kid screams, "I just saw your boy-tit!! You can't be a mermaid. You are a man." Then he starts chanting in that singsong voice every kid seems to know from birth. "You are a ma–an, You are a ma-an, You are a ma-an."

The entire park was full of preschoolers. And as soon as they heard someone being mocked, they swarmed towards the trailer like sharks that smell blood in the water. "You are a ma-an, You are a ma-an ..."

I have a good comeback for any situation: drunk hecklers, stupid frat boys ... but how do you tell a bunch of preschoolers to shut the fuck up?

TED: And I thought drag queens were cruel.

NATASHA: Everyone said showbiz would be hard. And if the whole thing had stayed a secret, that would've been the end of it. But the next day — it was on the front page of the entertainment section.

TED: Wait — I think I saw that —

NATASHA: And then there was a video clip on the six o'clock news.

TED: Oh my god, that was you?!?

NATASHA: Yeah. It went viral. Eighteen million hits. And now every time I walk into the Magical Crystal Palace, all the other queens chant "You are a ma-an, You are ..."

TED: You shouldn't have to put up with that.

NATASHA: Well, I wanted to be famous. Careful what you wish for.

TED: That doesn't mean you signed up to be bullied.

NATASHA: I'm a big girl. I can handle it.

TED: All you did was put your head above the crowd. You shouldn't be punished for that. This is why I spend all my time trying to blend into the background.

I'm glad I headed out tonight. Even if this is as far as I could get in my — adventure.

NATASHA: So am I.

Sometimes you gotta step up to the plate, Teddy. Do something that scares you. For you, it's giving up your "trappings" and setting out on your own. For me, it's getting in front of everyone and showing them what I am. WHO I am.

TED: You don't seem like you would scare easy.

NATASHA: Hence the outfit. I gotta go big or go home.

TED: Who gets to be the queen if you don't show up?

NATASHA: Lady Elaine. She's a total whore. And my best friend. The old troll. If it weren't for her backup dancers, they would boo her off the stage.

TED: Who are your backup dancers?

NATASHA: I don't have any. We got in a huge argument last week — something about artistic differences —

TED: Differences?

NATASHA: I thought they weren't working hard enough, and they thought I was a pushy bitch.

TED: You should never upset your backup dancers. Even I know that.

NATASHA: Whatever. I don't need them. I don't need anybody. I can do this routine blindfolded.

TED: Maybe — I could —

NATASHA: What?

TED: Never mind. Doesn't matter unless we get out.

NATASHA: Were you gonna say —?

TED: Nothing.

NATASHA: Nice try, Teddy. Show me those moves again.

TED: Nah, I don't —

NATASHA: SHOW ME!

He does them perfectly.

NATASHA: Oh my god. Perfect.

TED: Really? Thanks!

NATASHA: You're a natural. How come I never thought of it before?

TED: Thought of — what?

NATASHA: You have to be my backup dancer.

TED: What? No, I —

NATASHA: You have the right style — and you already know the moves —

TED: I couldn't.

NATASHA: You can!

TED: I shouldn't.

NATASHA: But you just did!

TED: People will laugh.

NATASHA: No, they'll cheer!

TED: They will?

NATASHA: You ever heard applause that's just for you? It's the most beautiful sound ...

TED: Yeah?

NATASHA: It would mean so much to me, Ted. Please.

He considers it. He moves forward, and the faint strains of the disco beat and the applause can be heard. Natasha realizes her boob has activated her iPod and turns it off.

TED: Tell you what — yes.

NATASHA: Yes?

TED: I'll do it!

NATASHA: Oh my god, that would save me. You have no idea.

TED: I'll be nervous.

NATASHA: I'll talk you through it. Now — let's get out of here. Mommy has a tiara to tackle! A crown to capture! A headpiece to hook! Let me boost you up.

TED: What?

NATASHA: Open that panel and look through it.

TED: I'm not climbing into an elevator shaft!

NATASHA: Just look. Maybe you can see something.

TED: Well ... Okay.

She boosts him up handily. He knocks the panel open and sticks his head through.

NATASHA: What do you see?

TED: An elevator shaft. It's dark.

NATASHA: What else?

TED: What am I supposed to be looking for?

NATASHA: A way out!

TED: It's kinda scary in here. And it smells. Let me down!

NATASHA: Look for anything unusual.

TED: Does a drag queen dressed as a Christmas tree holding up a man having a panic attack count?

NATASHA: Depends on where you're viewing it from, darling.

TED: That's not funny! Down! Please!

NATASHA: Wow. You're really shell-shocked.

She lets him down.

TED: So dark —

NATASHA: Here.

She takes off her headpiece and puts in on his head. It's way too big but stays on. She clicks the switch and it lights up.

NATASHA: Try again.

TED: But —

She ignores his protest and heaves him up again. He is less freaked out this time.

TED: Um — okay, I can see now —

NATASHA: What do you see?

TED: Nothing. Just the cables — some machinery — I don't know much about this stuff —

NATASHA: Anything that could help us?

TED: There's a screwdriver —

NATASHA: Perfect! Grab it!

TED: How will that help?

NATASHA: Just grab it!

He grabs it and she lowers him down. He hands her the screwdriver.

NATASHA: Oh my god, it's perfect.

TED: Can you get us out now?

NATASHA: No, but if I cover it in rhinestones, I have the perfect glamour mic for the show!

TED: What?

NATASHA: It's all part of the routine!

TED: For god's sake, FOCUS!

NATASHA: Oh. Right.

TED: What's the point? We're doomed. I'm doomed.

NATASHA: You give up too easy.

TED: Not everyone has a magical crystal palace to run off to.

NATASHA: Trust me — the name is pretty misleading.

She sprays her perfume again. Pause. He sniffs the air.

TED: That perfume is really —

NATASHA: Fabulous? Enticing? Mysterious?

TED: Strong.

NATASHA: Too much?

TED: No, it's kinda nice. Reminds me of —

NATASHA: Her?

TED: It's silly. I know.

NATASHA: No, not at all. Smell is a very powerful memory trigger. You can smell it now if you want.

TED: No, it's okay.

NATASHA: It'll cheer you up.

TED: No. It won't.

NATASHA: It will. I have some of it here —

TED: That's not — no, really, you don't have to —

NATASHA: Ah! There it is — I love this stuff.

She sprays a bit in the air, but it sprays right into Ted's eyes, and then the sprayer won't stop. It gushes wildly, filling the elevator. He starts flailing around in pain, gasping for air.

TED: AHHHHH!

NATASHA: Oh my god — what happened? Can you open your eyes?

TED: They're burning!

NATASHA: Take deep breaths!

TED: Can't — breathe —

NATASHA: I think I have a bottle of water in here —

TED: - choking —

NATASHA: Oh — never mind, it's Fruitopia —

TED: HURRY!

NATASHA: You want some?

TED: — allergic —

NATASHA: Oh my god, you're really sick aren't you?

TED: — fading —

NATASHA: I have to get us out. I'll get you out!

TED: — everything going black —

NATASHA: Hang on, Teddy Bear. I'll save us!

Using superhuman strength, she pries open the doors of the elevator. A loud alarm goes off. Lights flash. A siren blares.

The Magical Crystal Palace. The elevator has become the Disco Go-Go cage. A mirror ball drops from the ceiling. The elevator lights up like a dance floor.

The number starts. The two of them dazzle the crowd as they perform a fabulously choreographed routine. He is wearing rhinestone sunglass-

es and a tinsel headpiece. He does the backup vocals, while she carries the lead vocals. Her outfit has several "stages" that reveal and light up, and she has a solo or two playing the bells on her outfit, to thunderous approval.

The number ends and as Ted helps her reassemble her look, an announcer's voice is heard.

EMCEE: And now — the New Christmas Queen of the Magical Crystal Palace: NATASHA!!!

Thunderous applause and cheering. A crown and banner descend from the sky — flowers appear. She is in her glory. She waves to her public. The crowd chants, "You are The Queen! You are The Queen!" They adore her. The applause rings on and on. Lights slowly fade on her moment of triumph. The applause roars in the blackout.

DING!

Lights snap up to reveal the characters riding in the elevator. She is wearing her crown and a banner that reads Christmas Queen. *His jacket is draped over her shoulders. He is still wearing the glasses and pieces of his show outfit and carrying her bag. They are both struggling to contain their excitement as they replay the highlights in their minds.*

DING!

TED: You were amazing. Fabulous!

NATASHA: *You* were. That was some serious dancing.

TED: It felt good.

NATASHA: It sure did.

TED: The applause.

NATASHA: It was like thunder.

TED: Lightning.

BOTH: "The way you love me is frightening!"

Pause. ***DING!***

NATASHA: They loved the headpiece.

TED: They loved the lights. They loved you.

NATASHA: They loved *us*.

TED: They did.

Pause. ***DING!***

NATASHA: The bouncer thought your sunglasses were cute.

TED: Yeah? (*He takes off the glasses.*)

NATASHA: How do they feel?

TED: Better. The burning finally stopped.

NATASHA: Good.

TED: I think the strobe lights helped.

Pause. ***DING!***

TED: So?

NATASHA: So what, Teddy Bear?

TED: So how did I do? Does tonight count as broadening my horizons?

NATASHA: Well, a broad was definitely involved ...

Pause. ***DING!***

TED: I can still smell the perfume.

NATASHA: Yeah, we should probably call someone about that. It could last for days.

TED: Good.

Pause. ***DING!***

TED: Long ride.

NATASHA: It always is.

Pause. ***DING!***

TED: Where are you going to put your crown?

NATASHA: On my mantle.

TED: You have a mantle?

NATASHA: It's — just a shelf, really.

Pause. ***DING!***

TED: Thanks for the night out.

NATASHA: It was fun!

TED: It was!

Pause. ***DING!***

NATASHA: You know —

TED: Yes?

NATASHA: My first show as Queen — for New Year's Eve — do you think —?

TED: I'd love to!

NATASHA: Great.

TED: Great.

Pause. ***DING!***

TED: Same song?

NATASHA: I'll teach you a new one.

TED: Perfect.

NATASHA: Okay.

TED: Okay.

Pause. ***DING!*** *They have arrived on the fourteenth floor. The doors open.*

TED: After you, my Queen.

NATASHA: Why thank you, kind sir.

They step out. They exchange the coat and the bag.

TED: I just wanted to say —

NATASHA: You've been really —

TED: — thanks.

NATASHA: — helpful.

BOTH: You're welcome.

The elevator door closes. The sound of the elevator fades as it descends.

TED: You have a fabulous evening, Natasha.

NATASHA: I already have, Teddy Bear.

She heads down the hallway, turning to wave before she disappears. Ted watches. Once alone, he finally takes off his wedding ring and puts it in his pocket. He turns to head to his own apartment. Just before he disappears, he does a little step and twirl.

Blackout.

THE EDMONTON QUEEN: THE FINAL VOYAGE

For Lulu LaRude (Charles McDuff Gillis).

These stories are ours as much as they are mine.

All I had to do was remember.

Like I could ever forget.

RON JENKINS

Director, Playwright
Former Artistic Director, Workshop West, 2000–2006

I FIRST met Darrin Hagen at the Edmonton Fringe in 1993. I was directing a production of Robin Fulford's *Steel Kiss* in the upstairs room at a bar on Whyte Avenue called Rebar. Darrin and his husband and producing partner Kevin Hendricks were producing a show called Guys In Disguise in the downstairs portion of the bar. A Drag Extravaganza. The show was a huge hit, with audiences lining up for hours to see the most epic drag performance in Alberta.

Darrin was — and still is — one of the most charismatic people I have ever met. He makes you feel instantly comfortable, important, seen, and valued. He is interested in you ... your story. And he shares who he is. His story. So you feel like you know him, in about five minutes, maybe sooner.

We became fast friends and professional colleagues. We worked together, hung out together, and talked a lot, about theatre, life — and played a ton of Hearts in this huge house on 80th Avenue in Edmonton, a grand Strathcona manor that was notorious in the neighbourhood for the stream of drag queens who had moved in and out over the years.

We were at an opening at the Citadel one night when Darrin told me he was writing a play about his family. His drag family. His Edmonton family. His Big Onion family. The Hole Family.

"We'll do it at the Fringe next year. Wanna direct?"

"Absolutely." We clinked our plastic opening-night wineglasses to seal the deal.

He had been writing these incredible portraits of the Hole Family. His Drag Mother Lulu and her progeny.

These snapshots were beautiful, eloquent, hilarious, and devastating. An incredible tribute to his girls, his sisters, these Queens of the Underground at a bar called Flashback.

Darrin wanted us to know this chosen family: his family. And to tell about a Queer kid from Rocky Mountain House (or as he lovingly calls it, Rotten Monkey House) who came to Edmonton and was adopted, loved, and changed by this unconventional family.

It was at the Big House on 80th that he started to read me these stories. And as beautiful and intriguing as they were, they weren't quite a play yet. In his quest to make it all about them, Gloria/Darrin was missing, and I felt the reason for telling these stories wasn't there yet. He had told me why, and it was evident in the portraits, but it wasn't in the play yet. I told him he needed to write the opening: how he arrived from his hometown, his transformation: Gloria's story; and the ending: the why. He resisted. I insisted.

A week later I came over to The Big House and Darrin read the whole of *The Edmonton Queen* for a few close friends. Darrin had taken my notes and crafted them into something beautiful and sublime. Gloria's story was there in all its glory. The lightning rod. Our way in ...

And then he read the ending.

And when he was finished ...

We were all weeping and sobbing. The ugly type of crying. Tears and snot. For a while uncontrollable.

And in the silence after we had finished the Ugly Cry, we all knew in that moment why Darrin had invited us to his house. And eventually, so did audiences in the theatre that summer of '96.

Why he had written and told us this story.

Why it was important.

Why it was a work of art.

We knew ...

Together ... in that moment. That Darrin had captured ...

The Invisible.

“We lived among you. We lived with abandon. We lived here in spite of the rules, in spite of ourselves. We lived fast and hard and dangerous lives, and most of you never noticed.

We lived.

The Legends of the Underground.”

And through this beautiful work of art …

… they live again.

PRODUCTION HISTORY

The Edmonton Queen: Not a Riverboat Story

Edmonton Fringe Festival (Guys In Disguise); holdovers at Theatre Network, 1996
Starring Darrin Hagen
Directed by Ron Jenkins
Visual aide by Mandy Kamp
Sound design by Darrin Hagen
Stage management by Neon
Elizabeth Sterling Haynes Award Winner: Outstanding New Fringe Work

***The Edmonton Queen,* 1999–2001**

First Night Festival (Rice Theatre, produced by Guys In Disguise), 1999
Edmonton Street Performers' Festival (Rice Theatre, produced by Guys In Disguise), 2000
Winnipeg Fringe Festival (produced by Guys In Disguise), 2000
Globe Theatre, Regina Sandbox Series (produced by Guys In Disguise), 2000
Edmonton Fringe Festival (produced by Guys In Disguise), 2001
Starring Darrin Hagen
Directed by Ron Jenkins
Sound design by Darrin Hagen
Lighting design by James Chipman (2000, 2001)
Stage management by Catherine Hedlin (1999), Shawna Murphy (2000), Gina Moe (2001)

The Edmonton Queen: The Final Voyage

Fringe Theatre Adventures (produced by Guys In Disguise), 2009
Starring Darrin Hagen
Directed by Gina Moe
Set and costume design by Robert Shannon
Lighting Design by Roger Schultz
Sound Design by Darrin Hagen
Stage Management by Neon
Hair and makeup by James Ross (Twiggy)

The Edmonton Queen: The 30th Anniversary Voyage

Edmonton Fringe Festival (Theatre Network, produced by Guys In Disguise), 2026
Starring Zachary Parsons-Lozinski
Directed by Darrin Hagen
Set and lighting designed by Andraya Diogo
Sound design by Darrin Hagen
Stage management by Neon

PRODUCTION NOTES

DIALOGUE in bold is intended to be spoken aloud to signal a change of scene or focus.

Image courtesy of Ian Jackson / EPIC Photography; used with permission

Image courtesy of Ian Jackson / EPIC Photography; used with permission

The stage goes black. Music fades. Gloria, posed in front of an epic throne, surrounded by black-and-white photos scattered all over the floor.

Every once in a while, a queen is born

Lights fade slowly up, revealing Gloria.

Whether through osmosis or immaculate misconception is still mostly a mystery, but they appear. Suddenly, and without warning, a new pretender to the throne stands in front of you.

But where do they come from? Genderfuck meteors flaming to earth? Crossdressers crawling from every crevasse in the country? Often, they mutate out of men from the most macho of environments. But what triggers it?

Well, for many, the transition is as swift as it is brutal and final. And it happens once a year.

Every year, on October 31, thousands of young prairie men cross the line for the one night a year that they're actually permitted to do so. They cross the line that was drawn in the sandbox in front of them at the age of two; the line that shapes their thinking, their manner, their insecurities, their stress, their career, their lives, their perception.

On Halloween, they cross that line, and for one night, they know.

They put on a dress.

And every year, some of those men don't return.

Because once they're on the other side, the world looks different. And they get hooked.

Whether it's because the world is too drab and hopeless, or because there are too many shackles, or because someone said "no" one too many times, or because you're too fem to fit, or because it makes your cock hard, or because you're too fabulously stylish and dramatic for your own good ...

You try it. You love it. You buy it.

Not just the outfit. The lifestyle.

You fall in love. With the woman in you.

And the man you thought you were will do anything to make her dreams come true.

It can happen to any man ... trust me.

These are my snapshots. If this were my mother's photo album, everything would be blown up to portrait size, mounted under sticky cellophane in chronological order, with little ballpoint labels telling you who's who.

But this is my family album. They're just snapshots, because at the time, I didn't think a full portrait was necessary. They're just snapshots, a little out of focus because it was all moving pretty fast. They're just snapshots, but there's thousands of them ... overflowing, spilling out of boxes and basements ... shining, perfect moments frozen forever like the river in winter.

This is not a riverboat story. It's my — actually, our — story. The Lucky Ones.

And it's all true. Mostly. Let's just say I didn't have to make anything up. All I had to do was remember.

Like I could ever forget.

None of the names have been changed, because there are no innocents, but occasionally the outfits I describe are nicer than what we were actually wearing.

The eighties sashayed past us in a crinoline haze ... a cloud of dreaming bigger than anyone ever should. Foam and fur and feathers and false lashes ... it was like living backstage with the Muppets, only they were more realistic. And we used way more foam.

Delusions of Grandeur dressed by Value Village.

Our enormous visions ... these tiny gowns.

Why should you listen to the story of our lives?

Well, because ... they're fabulous, darlings!

Once Upon a Time ...

Isn't that how all fairy tales start?

Back then, the Greyhound bus left Rocky Mountain House twice a day: seven a.m. and suppertime. Not being a morning person, my ticket was for the latter. That left time to pack, say goodbye to a friend, and go watch the North Saskatchewan River flow past.

My river.

Standing on the bridge, an illusion occurs. The water moving under the bridge makes it feel like the whole bridge is moving backwards. Suddenly, I'm Barbra Streisand on the boat in *Funny Girl,* holding that impossible long note.

In Rocky Mountain House, you don't tell people you listen to Barbra Streisand. Rocky Mountain House is cowboy country.

I took my report cards filled with praise, my journal full of secrets, and a love letter from an older man in Edmonton. The one that almost got me thrown out of the house.

An older man. He was thirty-two.

I wouldn't be needing these in my new life.

I ripped them to pieces, letting them spin and flutter toward the aquamarine river. It's the sediment from the mountains that makes it that colour, they say. The stuff it carries in it makes it beautiful.

Time to start over.

I watched the paper float away. I realized, of course, that I wasn't really leaving it behind … I was sending it along ahead of me. Wonder how long it would take to float to Edmonton? If only I had a boat. I knew where I would end up.

It wasn't until Mom and Dad were driving me to the bus station that it kind of sunk in: I was moving. For good. I was free.

Now, in a TV family, this would be where the father would impart some words of wisdom to the young man as the journey of life is embarked upon. But … that's not really the way Dad and I work. Instead, Dad stood holding my accordion while Mom's words echoed in Dad's silence …

You can be whatever you want to be in this life. Don't ever miss a chance to change the world.

I don't think she had any idea how literally I would interpret those words.

I got a hug from Mom, and Dad shook my hand.

It's a guy thing.

They knew I didn't fit in. They didn't know what to do about it, but they knew.

As the Greyhound pulled out of town, I saw the bridge that me and my high school buddies had decorated with spray-paint. Someone had scrawled *fag* over our artwork.

The Greyhound stopped at Alhambra, Leslieville, Benalto, Eckville, and Sylvan Lake. Stockwell country. Keegstra country. Eckville is just up the road from Caroline, where the Aryan Nations have a lovely farm.

I could've gotten there faster on the river. I could've floated into town.

But back then, I was a little more subtle.

At Red Deer, Calgary and Edmonton are exactly the same distance away. South was Stampede country. North was hockey town. I wasn't very good at hockey; I was more the figure skate-y type. But I had already played horsey and knew I wasn't very good at that. I could have turned south but ...

... the river runs north. And it's my river.

As the Greyhound pulled into Edmonton, the prairie sun was just setting, the skyline just lighting up. Downtown sat overlooking the North Saskatchewan, twinkling like a giant tiara. We crossed the river.

I was home.

I moved in with my aunt and got a job at a bookstore, but that's not important. I was free. I needed to find the fag bar. Now it's not like you can just walk up to a stranger and say, "Hey, where do all the homos in this town hang out?"

However, it is possible to get into a taxi and say, "Hey, where do all the homos in this town hang out?" They'll take you right to it.

Flashback (the fag bar, not the theatrical device)

... through the smoke a vision of well-dressed hell and carnival chaos pounded on my brain/lights flash/bodies flail/the dance floor/ the drugs/ the MEN/if this is the circus, sign me up and point me to the bearded lady ...

You should've seen it. To get in, all you had to be was well-dressed, superbly coifed, famous, infamous, filthy rich, devastatingly beautiful, near-naked, encased in plastic, dripping in chains, balanced on spikes that could kill, a fabulous dancer, an exhibitionist, a voyeur, a swinger, a drug dealer, sleeping with the deejay, a go-go speaker boy, a muscle boy, a pretty boy, a boy, a model, a punk rocker, a jock, a dyke, a fag, a faghag, a draghag, a fruit fly, straight, bi, celibate, sexy, aloof, brooding, mysterious, scary, extreme, tireless ...

Beat.

Well, you could be almost anyone, really. But you still had to be prepared to wait in a line stretching as far as the Foxy Lady Disco Dancing Lounge for an hour or more. And name-drop your way through the front door.

Unless you were a Queen.

If you were a Queen, you could show up whenever your nail polish finally dried, unfold yourself from the taxi, and waltz in the front door of the club, past the lineups, past the commoners, past the plebes who pay to party. And you could tell from the way their lips curled as you minced past that they were all envious of the ease of entry. The drama. Of Drag.

I crossed that line ... into the Underground ... away from the light of day ... forever.

My first Halloween at Flashback, I saw my first drag show. The crowd was jammed in around the stage. The lights went down, then a drumroll, and then …

My world exploded into a tornado of taffeta, sequins, lace, rhinestone earrings, grand, sweeping arm gestures, grand, sweeping eyelashes that sent breezes rippling to the back row, carried by the voices of Divas ripping through my soul, and suddenly, for the first time in this little boy's life, the world made sense.

It all made sense: wearing a towel on my head when I was four so I could pretend I had long hair; lip-synching into my hairbrush to my collection of albums, all girl singers, before I ever knew what drag music was; that teenage fantasy of being the fourth Charlie's Angel; that dream of standing on a stage with the applause ringing in my ears, except I never bowed to accept their praise, I curtsied …

None of that was a mystery anymore. Because I had seen myself on that stage that night. Glamorous … adored … powerful. One by one they dazzled the crowd: Janis Joplin, Princess Grace, Mama Cass, Marilyn Monroe, Tallulah Bankhead, Judy Garland!

Then, after the show, I watched the Queens. Their names filtered through the pounding disco: Bianca Bang-Bang, Amii L Nitrate, Lindee Starr, Mrs. K., Mary Mess, Reena Del Rocko, Boom-Boom Breezy: Roller-Derby Queen, Lexy Con, Ginger Snot, and my favourite: Felice Blabby-Blah … like codes to a more glamorous life.

It was the first time I saw men being anything other than manly and not get beat up for it. And in the back of my mind, I heard *her* voice as she began to take shape. What I had seen allowed *her* to be imagined. Nothing would ever be the same again. The world looked different.

Beat.

I gotta get me one of those names.

So I watched. Closely. There had to be one of them who could show me the ropes. It had to be someone worthy, because I knew I would be a fabulous Queen, once given the opportunity. Someone original, someone you couldn't take your eyes off, someone the same size as me so we could trade outfits, once I had some.

And then one night, she was standing in front of me.

She was partying with Trash, the reigning Mz. Flashback. The two of them were making a one-time appearance as neo-punk Valley Girls decorated with extension cords, held together with staples and safety pins. They floated through the club on a quaalude cloud, connected by cables and cords, outcasts from the glamour circuit, living a fashion anarchy. Their laughter at the crowd's confusion floated across the club ... it was music to my ears.

They were like me. Only free.

I asked the bartender her name.

Wha —? Oh, that's Lulu LaRude. Don't waste your time ... she's a ho. You could do so much better.

The crowd parted as she walked through. She was like a magical punk princess, with an aura that made her stand out in a mob of people desperate to stand out. She's looking at me. ... Oh my god, she's walking over here.

She towered over me and said, "You're new. But not for long."

The spell was cast. We went home and fucked, because that's how you met people back then.

In the beginning, there was Lulu LaRude.

ME: Lulu, why do you do drag?

LULU: A man in a dress learns more in a day than a man in a suit learns in a lifetime.

ME: But ... you're not like the other Queens.

LULU: Forego the Fabulous and Embrace Anarchy. You don't change the world by doing what it tells you to do.

It was gradually dawning on me that we weren't boyfriend material; we were girlfriend material.

ME: People tell me I'd look fabulous in drag.

LULU: I fuckin' knew it! Why does every boy I bring home wanna be a girl?

ME: I don't wanna be a girl, I just ... wanna do shows with you guys.

LULU: You have so much to learn. You can't just walk in and say, 'Hi! I just moved here from a trailer court in Rotten Monkey House and I'm a great big fag and can I be in the show?'

She went on to explain: the drag camp is a closely guarded one. Without a mother figure to take you under her hemline, you would merely float on the fringe, looking for a way into the scene. Outsiders themselves, Queens are by nature suspicious of outsiders.

I hung on her every word as she explained how she planned to rise to the heights of The Underground.

LULU: You gotta get a crown.

ME: How do you do that?

LULU: You do whatever it takes. It's just like a beauty pageant, but meaner. You have a choice between Entertainer of the Year, Mz. Flashback, and Empress.

Without a crown, you're just a pretender. Until they nail that rhinestone cookie cutter on your head, you're not a Queen. Otherwise you'll never get a high heel in the door. Got it?

ME: I think so. ... Why don't you have a crown?

LULU: I will. It's not as easy as it sounds. But I will be Empress of the Big Onion someday.

ME: Lulu, why do you call Edmonton the Big Onion?

LULU: 'Cause, sweetheart. Someday, it'll make you cry.

Every once in a while, a Queen is born.

Lulu adopted me that night, laying the seeds of a Royal Family that would rule The Big Onion for the next decade.

But I'm getting ahead of myself.

Was it just luck that her outfits all fit me perfectly? Both of us were tall and impossibly loud, like gigantic screaming Barbie dolls with no off button. Not to mention: size fourteen shoes.

ME: How do you walk in these?

LULU: Pretend you're on a tight rope. And the hips should be like Jell-O if it could walk.

ME: What do you mean?

LULU: If you have to ask, then we're wasting our time. Can you dance?

ME: In these? I doubt it.

LULU: Okay. We'll just worry about arm gestures for now. There are three basics: Love My Ceiling, Love My Drapes, and Love My Carpets. Go ahead, give it a shot.

Gloria tries them.

LULU: Oh, for Chrissakes, you're doing a drag number, not landing a plane. Flourish, sweetie! Flourish! Okay ... let's talk about drag music. A good drag number has funny lyrics. OR a disco beat. OR a kickline. OR a long note at the end. OR a false ending. OR you lip-synch to live recordings.

ME: How come?

LULU: Because, dear, that way if nobody claps, you will still hear applause.

The training began. I looked at Lulu in awe .... She loved life on the edge. It was where she did her best work. I would watch her painting her makeup, memorizing the many phases of faces.

ME: What are you doing with that glue stick?

LULU: Erasing my eyebrows.

ME: Why?

LULU: So I can draw them on where I want.

ME: Oh ... Now what are you doing?

LULU: Contouring. You can change the shape of your face. See? Cheekbones.

ME: Cool. Um ... does it all really have to be that thick?

LULU: I'm a Queen, not a schoolgirl. It takes more than an oatmeal scrub and a dusting of blush to pull it off. This is no time for subtlety.

ME: What do you make tits out of?

LULU: That, my dear, depends on the dress. Unpopped popcorn kernels in nylons are good 'cause they're moldable, but heavy. Water balloons jiggle really nice, but they can pop without warning. I use my socks. That way I know where they are at the end of the evening.

ME: How come so many pairs of nylons?

LULU: It's either that or shave my legs. Any other questions? Great. Call a cab. I have to go tuck.

ME: What's a tuck?

LULU: It's how you hide your dick when you're in spandex. It's kind of like a sandwich baggie: Flip, Flop, Fold the Top. How do I look?

ME: I can see the hair on your back.

Beat.

LULU: Shut up and hand Mommy that razor.

I would drop her off at the Strip by the Holiday Inn where the hookers plied their trade, and wait for her to meet me later at the bar, where she would tell me tales of perverts and freaks. One of her favourite lines, once she had the trick's money, was, "By the way, I'm a queen ... I hope you don't mind."

Most of them didn't. Men usually don't.

One day, in one of our rare daylight moments, Lulu and I sat on a low brick wall, watching the endlessly boring K-Days parade schlep past. It was about to rain, as it always did, and we were bored, as we usually were. We passed a joint back and forth, giggling about how funny straight people were when they tried to stage a big event. The most glamorous thing we had seen so far was the Klondike Kate convertible, and frankly, we had better fashion sense.

LULU: Look! It's like Laura Ingalls wearing a toilet paper cozy!

Suddenly we heard a scream from about three blocks away. Not a scream of fear or warning as much as a scream of announcement, of arrival. Everyone around us looked in the direction of the scream.

She was walking towards us, in a drugged-out crinoline cloud, feathers in her hair, dress cut down to there, a banner across her foamies that read Clone Dyke Queen.

LULU: Oh my God, it's Trash!

Lulu and Gloria both cheer madly.

She heard us screaming and joined us on the wall.

TRASH: I did a hit of acid and decided it was a good day for a parade. Who knew there was already one happening? So I just joined in. Girl, you should have seen the cute boy I had my picture taken with back there ...

I was skeptical. I never thought Trash looked that convincing. But as I sat there, disbelieving, Lulu shushed both of us. "Jocks in convertibles: three o'clock."

A moment of reverent silence as the beefcake float drove closer.

"Chomp." "Chomp." "Oh my god — chomp!"

They were Oilers or Eskimos or something butch like that, I've never been able to tell them apart. Just as they got to right about here, Trash screamed, "Hi, honey! Give a girl a lift?"

The jocks all looked in her direction and waved, and then one of them motioned for her to get in. "That's my cue, see ya later!"

Trash jumped off the low wall, navigated through a bunch of kids, then trotted as fast as she could manage after the motorcade, as Lulu and I sat silent, our jaws hanging wide open.

The jock's face changed expression gradually as Trash drew closer. Remember, distance is a girl's best friend. Up-close drag reality in daylight is a sobering experience.

No one can blend that well.

By the time the jock figured out what he was dealing with, it was too late. Trash had climbed into the convertible and sat high on the back, waving like the perfect pageant winner. Short of physically tossing her onto the asphalt, there wasn't a lot he could do.

As they drove away, we saw Trash put her gloved hand on the jock's knee. He did nothing; just sat, staring straight ahead as his buddies howled with laughter.

Lulu and I sat in awe. "Go, girl," we whispered with admiration. Silently, we saluted, giving the Royal Wave: hat-two-three, purse-two-three, pearls-two-three, wave, and rest.

To both of us, Trash was a vision of the future of drag: bravado, balls, and a utilitarian fashion sense that appealed to our beer-bottle ballgown budget. As my dragmother's sister, she inspired a certain respect. Plus she had the Mz. Flashback crown. She was our way in. The three of us became inseparable, inspiring each other to new heights of lunacy. We were the Sisterhood of Unrecognized Royalty.

All we needed was a palace befitting our delusions of grandeur.

Trash phoned one day and told us she had found it.

A drag house is an easy one to spot. It will be a large, prominent structure, corner lot, probably with a dramatic entrance or turret or balcony or something fabulous about it. Chances are, if it looks like a costume epic could be filmed in the front yard, it's rented by Queens.

Never just one; always a pack.

Lulu came up with the name for our new abode: West Walla Walla Guatemala Falklands Mall, soon shortened to Walla Walla West. With a month, the address could make a cabby quake with fear.

Two other Queens moved in with us as well. Prickles worked at Earl's and drank way too much, but was almost never there, which suited us fine. Iona Box was a post-apocalyptic pseudo-punk poet who donned the occasional frock, when the occasion demanded. Iona immediately insisted that we take down all the porcelain Pierrot clowns that Lulu collected. Iona had a phobia about clowns; they gave her nightmares.

Beat.

She had never been to a MacDonald's for that very reason.

Within days the house was filling up. Walla Walla West was a workshop/warzone.

Trash collected garbage, which is how she got her name, and turned it into stunningly bizarre *objets d'art*. Lulu collected piles of drag in every room, Prickles collected liquor bottles, I had sheet music all over my piano, and Iona wrote poetry. The poetry multiplied on doors, mirrors, and counters; you'd find it in your drag bag, in your bed, in your closet. My piano bench filled up with paper filled with Iona's scribblings.

Here's one of my favourites:

The OK Cat

By Iona Box

She seemed like an OK cat.

But at night, when no one was looking…

… she beat her kittens.

The End

I did my first drag show around then.

I was a tall, stunning goddess in spandex and gold lamé, wowing the crowd with my first-timer chutzpah.

I can say that because none of you were there. There are no videos. There are no photos (well, one, but I haven't seen it in a decade, so it's probably lost by now). There is no one to dispute my version of events.

I was stunning. It was everything I'd ever dreamed it could be and more electrifying than I'd ever hoped.

It scared the shit out of me, it was that good. I'd finally found my drug. Real life was nothing ... this was the thrill I'd been preparing for from day one.

When my eyes locked with her eyes in the mirror, and for a moment, everything else disappeared. I saw someone looking back, a total stranger that I recognized immediately. I saw my sister, myself, the only woman that will ever understand me. A combination of my mother, the wife I'll never have, the woman I'll never be.

... I fell in love with her that night ... and I fell hard. I had never met anyone like her.

But I was still without a name. We had tried out several, but none stuck. I was Mount St. Helen for a week, but then the volcano blew and the joke was over, so that was no good. Then I was Naomi Fuckstick, which I hated, which is a bad thing, `cause if you hate a drag name bad enough, it'll stick forever.

ME: Lulu, why can't I just pick my own name?

LULU: Yeah, right. Then it'll be something stupid like Crystal or Caress. It has to be unique.

ME: But there's another show coming up. It would be nice to be able to be introduced as ... something.

LULU: The wrong name can sink you. It has to set a tone. And you'll be stuck with it forever, so we have to choose carefully.

Then, without warning, Trash and Lulu woke me up in the middle of the night. They blindfolded me, dragged me out of the house. In a secret sacred ceremony, we took a dip in the fountain at the Legislature, lit a joint off the eternal flame, and Trash and Lulu anointed me with the name that would immortalize me underground for eternity. Lulu solemnly touched each of my shoulders with The Rhinestone Turkey Baster. I took a toke, held my breath, and waited for the name.

LULU: I dub thee: GLORIA HOLE.

ME: What?

TRASH: Gloria Hole. It's fabulous.

LULU: Trash thought of it. Isn't it fabulous?

TRASH: It's you! It's fabulous.

ME: But I was kinda hoping for something more ... dignified.

LULU: Get over yourself, honey. Dignity is something you earn. You have so much to learn.

TRASH: You know, we could just go back to calling you Naomi Fuckstick.

ME: No, no, no ... Gloria's fine. But ... Hole?

LULU: It's funny.

ME: It's gross.

LULU: Mark my words, Gloria. The Hole Family will be a mighty name in this town someday.

In the beginning, there was Lulu LaRude. Lulu LaRude begat Gloria Hole.

Swept up in the Delusion of Grandeur of the moment, I vowed to uphold the Hole Family name, and to work tirelessly towards the advancement of the Hole Family name.

We were Dragon Queens. Together, we made a pact; we would be next. Together, we could rule this town. The Big Onion was ours for the taking.

Well, almost. This game was ruled by tradition. Like any age-old ritual, it had rules, protocol, and etiquette. We had to be crowned to make it official. Crowns garnered respect.

This was not gonna be easy ... Lulu needed a real job (hooker didn't look good on the application for Empress), and I ... well, frankly, I was merely a dragling. We just weren't crown material.

Yet.

Our first show was called "The Wild Sorority Sisters from the Planet Playtex Proudly Present: A Salute To Trailer Court Women." It was the first in a long line of demented performances that would launch us into infamy.

Lulu ran for Empress but lost. Either she or the world wasn't ready yet. So we launched into plan B: our official arrival: May long weekend. The Coronation of the ninth Mz. Flashback.

I became that Mz. Flashback.

And when they put that crown on my head, and when I fastened it on for every special appearance for the next year, I was one of the Lucky Ones; the Outcast Elite.

Queen of the Underground! A Legend in her own Lunchtime!

From that point on, we performed like our lives depended on it. It was us they came to see: the Stars of the Underground.

And we never disappointed.

Monday to Friday was spent planning, rehearsing, trying on, colour draping, shoplifting and stockpiling narcotics. Even if you weren't planning to crank, dressing up was a major event. We had reputations to uphold. It was our responsibility to be bigger than life, and we took that challenge seriously. The plebeians depended on us.

This is not something that just came about randomly. Our schedule was strict, the itinerary regimented:

FRIDAY

2:00 p.m.	Awake.
4:00 p.m.	Awake again. Get up.
4:30 p.m.	Remove last night's makeup.
5:30 p.m.	Put on makeup to cover makeup that won't come off. Go buy cigarettes.
6:30 p.m.	Count the acid. Plan the dose.
7:30 p.m.	Awake again. Your cigarette has burned a hole in the couch.
8:30 p.m.	Put on the worn-out scratched version of Bette Midler's Divine Madness to get in the mood. Remove makeup. Shave. Moisturize. Begin applying Night Makeup.
10:30 p.m.	Face completed. Search drag room for anything to wear.

GLORIA: Lulu! What are you wearing?

LULU: You can't wear my palazzo pants.

GLORIA: As if I would.

LULU: I'm doing the black shimmy-fringe number.

GLORIA: With or without the vinyl purse?

LULU: Without.

GLORIA: I left my purse at the club. Can I —?

LULU: Fine. Just don't lose it again.

GLORIA: Why can't I wear your palazzo pants?

LULU: It would look like a slipcover on you.

GLORIA: But it matches the purse.

GLORIA: Find Lulu's black shimmy-fringe for her. Secretly pick out the silver lamé palazzo pants for yourself.

11:30 p.m. Light a joint. Call a cab. Take the first hit of acid. Lulu is practising her next drag number in the mirror upstairs.

11:35 p.m. Last-minute costume change. Palazzo pants are so retro — What was I thinking?? ... Decide instead on the standard rich hooker ensemble. But this needs the black patent Joan Crawford come-fuck-me pumps, which are buried in the attic. Start to dig. Lulu begins to reconsider her whole genderfuck punk goddess motif and starts eyeing the silver lame palazzo pants. She goes to try them on.

11:45 p.m. Cab arrives. You don't hear him honking 'cause you and Lulu are fighting over the silver beaded purse.

11:50 p.m. Emerge from the house wearing Lulu's punk goddess motif, she in the silver lamé palazzo pants. Fold yourself into the taxi: "Careful! The hair!" The bigger the hair, the closer to God.

11:55 p.m. Spend the entire ride downtown trying to keep Lulu from hitting on the cabbie. Some girls just don't know when to quit.

MIDNIGHT: ARRIVE! Step out of the taxi, overtip the driver for not punching us out, adjust your miniskirt to hide the run in your nylons, scream with joy, look down your nose at the poor hetero commoners in the lineup, breeze past them, say hi to the Reverend Bob as he buzzes you in, push through the crowd, dump your furs in the office, sneak up behind a bartender, grab his ass, "Free-pour me a scotty, don't bruise the ice like you did me last time. Don't you look sassy. Boyfriend out of town again? Make it a quadruple and I won't tell him a thing. Just put that on my tab. Where are the girls standing? Oh! Stop looking, I found them." Strut through the crowd, receive compliments, "Excuse me, pardon me, excuse me, thank you, Hi, hi there, Oh, thank you, this old thing? Aren't you sweet? Yeah, your dress is really nice too ... fuck, who let all the straight chicks in? It's like a Mary Kay graduation. Look, they all dance the same, watch this watch this: boing, boing, turn around, boing, boing, turn around. Oh my god, I love this song! Let's dance. Who's got the poppers, no, up here, I want everyone to see this outfit. Get off the speaker, bitch, we live here! God where did all these Barry T's wannabes come from? It's like being at the mall, only hideous. Donna Summer is so fabulous, isn't she? I know we're supposed to hate her now, but the MUSIC!"

12:45 a.m. Time for more acid. Meet in the wheelchair stall in the ladies' can at the prearranged time. Squeeze everyone in. Sit on the floor, screaming with laughter at absolutely anything. Pass around the hairspray. Stay until some serious lesbian kicks you out, claiming that you're reinforcing negative stereotypes of women. "Oh yeah? Well, at least we're not reinforcing negative stereotypes of farmers!" Leave in a huff.

1:00 a.m. Get that feeling in your stomach that lets you know your drugs are kicking in. "Another scotch, queen size, please." Lulu's drinking beer out of the bottle with a long straw so she doesn't mess up her lipstick. Sit high on the bar with your legs crossed so you can torment the straight boys. Watch the dance floor flicker and flash and flex and fascinate. Cheer with Lulu as two guys climb up on a speaker start tearing off each other's clothes. The club is full, and the beautiful people keep pouring through the door. Some cute guy can't take his eyes off your tits, so take one out and pat his forehead dry.

1:15 a.m. Hallucinate. Lulu's talking about something, screaming in your ear. Nod and pretend you understand her. The cute guy is now licking your legs. You feel too sorry for him to tell him that you can't feel a thing because you're wearing four pairs of Shopper's Drug Mart pantyhose.

1:30 a.m. Ditch the guy. Find the Girls.

1:45 a.m. Grab Lulu and head to the walk-in beer cooler. Take off your shoes and stand on the cold steel until the swelling in your feet goes down. Once shoes fit again, renew dancing.

2:00 a.m. Last call. Ignore it. You know management.

2:30 a.m. Whine to management for more scotch. Hang out with the bartenders in the office while they count their tips. Make so much noise they kick you out. Leave in a huff.

3:00 a.m. Start looking for a party. If unsuccessful reconvene in the wheelchair stall and start your own.

3:30 a.m. Hang out in the kitchen, even though the lighting is brutal. Last song is playing, and the hundreds of party animals start lining up for their coats. Get more scotch.

4:00 a.m. Decide against calling a cab. You and Lulu have decided, in your stoned wisdom, to walk home. Head down Jasper Avenue, still in heels, arm in arm, the morning sun revealing the stubble growing through the all-night makeup. Beat up a gang of six straight guys who think fags won't fight back. They soon learn that I'm from Rocky Mountain House ... and Lulu's from Cape Breton.

4:30 a.m. Go into the Mac's store and call a cab, even though Walla Walla West is only a block away. Buy cigarettes and wait in the store for our cab. The guy behind the counter asks if we would please wait outside. We ask him if he would please fuck off. Leave in a huff.

5:00 a.m. Go to bed. Have trouble sleeping. You're not sure if it's from the acid, or the uppers, or the downers, or the black eye.

SATURDAY: Rinse. Repeat.

Rise of a Drag Dynasty

The Flashback stage was mine now. Plus I had to represent the club at any drag extravaganza I could scrape enough money to travel to. My first official appearance as the new Mz. Flashback was at the Calgary Ball. Lulu displayed me proudly, like a new pair of earrings. It was at that same ball that Lindee Starr sold Entertainer of the Year to Lulu as they stole the Empress of Vancouver's rhinestone necklace from the trunk of a car. When Lulu told me, I thought she was joking.

But that summer, Lulu was crowned Entertainer of the Year, just as promised. Halfway through her number, her wig fell off. She plunked it back on her head without missing a beat. The crowd roared.

That crown meant that Lulu was now accepted by the Dowagers. Between us, we had two crowns. Now she could run for Empress. There would be no stopping us.

Two weeks later, one of her lungs collapsed as we hot-knifed hash in the drag room. She went into the hospital for surgery. The timing couldn't have been worse — Lulu's campaign for Empress was merely a month away. She got out of the hospital just in time for the first campaign show. She stepped on stage in a full-length gown to hide the bandages.

She never wore backless again.

Lulu LaRude was crowned Empress IX in the Ballroom at the Holiday Inn, right on the corner of boredom and desperation where she used to work the streets. The ballroom erupted with a roar of approval, she entered, the spotlight hit her, her beaded gown lit up the sky. She beamed radiantly, like a monarch filled with love for her children, her people, that moment ...

... that shining perfect moment ...

That crown belonged there.

At the Victory Brunch the next day, Lulu announced the name of her Royal Court: the Ninth Imperial House of Dirty Diamonds. Then, she broke with tradition, and instead of promoting the loser, Lori St. John, she appointed me her Imperial Crown Princess. Second in line to the throne. And then she did something no Empress had ever done. Lulu gazed at me in Motherly wisdom. "I've decided the Royal Family will be named after you."

The Hole Family. The whole Hole Family. Named after me.

The Hole Family had arrived. There would be no turning back.

And to the victor go the Goils. We were suddenly surrounded by Queens eager to share the edges of that spotlight, as they simultaneously plotted to wear the crown next. An embarrassment of bitches started hanging out at Walla Walla West, which became an orphanage, attracting wayward homeless homos from all over Canada.

Lulu started selecting her court from amongst the intriguers, as a stirring of Motherly instinct tugged at my cotton gusset.

My biological clock was ticking; drag time meant it was bit behind schedule, but better late than never. I was halfway through my year as Mz. Flashback, and it was time to start thinking about finding a successor, someone who would let us retain control. I took an interest in a fascinating work in progress. I was ready for my first child.

Lulu LaRude begat Gloria Hole begat Tallulah.

For Tallulah, life was full of firsts. Growing up in the tundra, she had missed some fairly commonplace rites of passage for Canadian boys.

Growing up nearly blind can't be easy. Growing up a nearly blind overweight epileptic homo, next to impossible.

Yet ... there she stood: jaw and cheekbones sharp enough to slice bagels, eyes painted à la silent movie star, with a Cleopatra wig framing her face. You didn't have to scratch much of the paint off to find that terrified Tundra Fairy underneath ... but she was rapidly becoming a crowd favourite, blossoming under the care of their applause.

I tried to talk Tallulah into running for Mz. Flashback 10. She was very reluctant, but once I convinced her that Lulu and I would do everything for her, she agreed. It was an easy win ... the timing was perfect. I placed that crown on her head lovingly, the way my dragmother had shown me.

Flashback: The fag bar AND Flash forward (the theatrical device)

The drag room. A long mirrored tunnel under the sound booth filled with skinny pasty boys. None of us ever saw the light of day. The only colour in our cheeks was the stuff we painted on.

It's a big night. Lulu is stepping down as Entertainer of the Year. This crown was a special one, and you couldn't run for it — you had to be chosen. Who received the glory next was entirely up to her. And she wasn't talking.

Who would she choose? We were all in the running. Tallulah? Twiggy?

Me?

The show is already an hour late. Out in the bar, nobody notices.

Nerves frazzle on contact. All are applying makeup. Fanning lashes to dry the glue. Slipping on pair after pair after pair of nylons. In the hairspray/face-powder/perfume/cigarette-smoke/body-odour-choked air, curses and giggles and boyisms and girlisms bounce off the makeup mirror. Queens are mean, but before they take it out on you, they warm up on each other.

Tallulah was a changed queen. In one year, the boy who had to be talked onto the stage had become gutsy, daring, and original. She was doing Grace Jones for the first time.

Now, watching a five foot ten pretty boy transform himself into an avant-garde Glamazon takes some imagination in the early phases.

First: Erase the face. Glue painted over the brows. Avocado green beard cover. (Tallulah was Italian. Three words: one o'clock shadow.)

Then a thick thick thick layer of base. No, thicker.

Then: powder, powder, powder, powder, pack it in, pack it in, powder, powder, powder, powder, pack it in pack it in pack it in.

Now of course, Tallulah had serious issues with her vision. In her male guise she wore thick black glasses and couldn't see much without them. This makes eye makeup particularly challenging.

So she had developed a routine: draw one third of an eyebrow. Sit back. Put the glasses on. Lean in. Take the glasses off. Draw another third of an eyebrow. Sit back. Put the glasses on. Lean in. Take the glasses off. Draw another third of an eyebrow. Light a smoke. This dance repeated for every step of the dozens of steps that comprise a dynamic drag eye. The eye has to be delicious. Or go home. It's worth taking your time.

And, as usual, Tallulah was behind schedule. And crabby.

Iris floats in. Late. Lulu bitches at her because it's her show and she can, plus Iris always kind of inspires that kind of abuse. We call her Virus.

There's no room for Iris at the head mirror (well, there is, but we don't really want her there), so we send her back to get ready by the janitor sink we all pee in before the show. Definitely B-list.

Twiggy arrives. Also late, but we like her. Slender, sophisticated, sparkly. Our star dancer. She does things in heels that no woman would dare. We make room at the head mirror. Definitely A-list.

Tallulah has moved on to black liner. First the pencil, to sketch it in. Top lid. One third at a time. The glasses. Light a smoke. Everyone is many steps ahead of her in prep but she won't speed up. Lean in. Glasses off.

The show is now two hours late. Out in the bar, nobody notices.

Twiggy's gossiping about Iris. Turns out when Iris's roommate, Lori St. John, was in the hospital, Iris pawned off all the furniture, appliances, even the fish tank. None of which belonged to her. She was probably wearing the profits right now in the form of that new beaded disaster of a gown she arrived in, illustrating once more that taste and price don't always travel together.

This amuses all of us greatly, except Tallulah who's just in a pissy mood. The bar owner calls down to the drag room because people are asking when the show is gonna happen. He is met with a confused chorus of lies about their total near-readiness.

Everyone looks at Tallulah. She has moved on to eyelashes. This is where it gets complicated because on top of not being able to see with no glasses, she has to partially close one eye at a time and watch what she's doing with her other eye. First the left. A bit of glue. Wait for it to get tacky. Then slowly — first attempt goes horribly wrong. Glue in the eye. Tallulah swears. She throws the tube of glue at the mirror. She gets up and heads to the janitor sink to take a pee and calm down.

Then Twiggy prances out for a shooter at the bar. Then Tallulah storms back in a rage because Iris won't move to let her piss. Then the door flies open and Twiggy appears with a wild panicked look and is about to say something, some kind of warning, when she trips on her marabou cape and plunges in a sparkling heap to the foot of the stairs. We all jump up and run to her. We form a circle to pick her up and get her to a chair. Her ankle is fucked.

And just as we heave — the door opens again and two police officers step into the drag pit.

The room falls completely silent except for the subtle crinkle of plastic as someone discreetly tucks a bag of pot into a bra. Eight queens in various states of readiness, most in nothing more than pantyhose and dance belts, almost all with some kind of outstanding warrant, look up at them.

The cops scan the room. The eyes looking back at them are heavy, dark, harshly powdered. You can never wear too much Bridget Bardot Black.

Lulu makes a "yummy, yummy" kind of predatory noise at the back of her throat. It's for cop number two, a strapping tall young blond demigod in uniform. Lulu lights up a cigarette, squeezes a breast into shape and strikes a pose. She steps up to them, all seven feet and two hundred-plus pounds of her. She towers over both of them, completely filling the space between floor and ceiling. She gazes down at the older cop's bald spot and exhales into that already-smoky air.

She purrs, "Well, if it isn't the husbands. I love a man in uniform — as long as he's got fifty bucks. Whatcha lookin' for, boys?"

In his best official unflustered voice, cop number one, an older married seen-it-all kind of guy, says, "We're looking for a Mister ______" ... and then he says a man's name.

Understand, for a moment, that in the drag world, boy names just never came up. We had spent years as Twiggy, Gloria, Lulu, Tallulah. It's all we knew. So it took a moment. To register.

Then a collective rush of realization: they were looking for Iris.

Everyone goes on naïve mode. We've got the home advantage. We know that even if Iris walks into the room, she's in drag. They won't recognize her. Unless someone tells.

It's an interesting position to be in. We could pull the wool over the eyes of Edmonton's finest. That would be cool. Or we could send Iris off to spend the night in jail. In drag.

Also cool.

And just as we all ponder what not to say, Tallulah screamed, "Virus, there's some visitors here for you."

There's something titillating about watching a lanky blond cop handcuff a drag queen. Even when it's Iris. There, but for the grace of God ...

As the cops dragged Iris away, Lulu screamed some Motherly advice: "Remember what I taught you Virus — you know your rights. You're entitled to one phone call AND a strip search!"

Iris didn't do the show that night. She spent the next twelve hours in a holding cell in full gear. Not an experience for the faint of heart. The lighting is merciless and by the time you're processed, your beard is growing through.

Or, at least, that's what I've heard.

Twiggy did do the show that night. Fucked ankle and all. She changed into something floor-length, we carried her to centre stage, and she did a Streisand stand-and-quiver kind of performance. The audience cheered, she bowed, and we carried her off.

Tallulah would have done the show that night, but by this time she was so far behind schedule and so stressed out that none of us should have been surprised when her epileptic seizure started. At the mirror she dropped her black liner, her hand started to vibrate, then her arm spasmed and she fell back in her chair, pulling the makeup counter over on her way down. She's on the floor in a pile of tackle boxes and colour palettes, doin' the old gran mal.

The six remaining Queens start screaming and running around. Red Cross hadn't taught blending, so none of us went.

"Is there a doctor in the house???"

In comes a leather queen in full gear. Who knew those outfits came with stethoscopes?

An hour later she was driven home wrapped in a bathrobe, where she slept for two days. I ended up wearing her Grace Jones earrings for my number.

Beat.

Well, *she* wasn't gonna need them.

Despite all the chaos backstage, we all performed our asses off that night. I became the newest Entertainer of the Year. The crowning, when it finally happened, ended up going on three and a half hours late.

Out in the bar, nobody noticed.

Lulu and I shared a quiet moment in the drag pit after the crowning.

LULU: This is it. This is your last crown. Unless you run for Empress.

GLORIA: Too much protocol. I can't kiss ass like you do.

LULU: I'll take that as a compliment. Well, then, we have to groom the next successor.
As the web of power spread, the pressure to sustain that power multiplied.

Life was a zoo; we were the keepers and the main attraction. Ever since we had been crowned, we had been surrounded by other people. The bills at Walla Walla West mounted ... we ignored them. Our lives had become a hurricane of shows, appearances, trips out of town, calming Queens down, fixing internal Family issues, choosing successors, banishing anyone who pissed us off ... It took a lot of energy.

Heavy lies the wig that wears the crown.

Then ... we stepped down, sashaying as graciously as we could into the hallowed ranks of The Hall of Dowagers. Act One of Lulu's ball was a bridal theme; I was the bridesmaid ... she was the bride.

For her final walk as Empress, she performed "You Are My Friend" by Patti Labelle and dedicated it to me.

But the Hole Dynasty flourished. Lulu and I were both Dowagers when Tallulah gave birth to her first daughter, my granddaughter, Lulu's great-granddaughter, the one who, right from the start, seemed destined for a new kind of immortality.

Lulu LaRude begat Gloria Hole begat Tallulah begat Ora Fice

Ora was a strange creature: devious, ambitious, desperately seeking something. In the early years you could watch Ora soak up information like a makeup sponge. She would see what worked and steal it. People were tools of the trade for her — Friends as Fodder for Fame.

Ora was also the queen of costume interruptus. At the Christmas show, she walked onto the stage decorated like a tree. The tinsel and twinkling lights looked great until she started dancing. Then mayhem struck: glass balls shattering and popping as they gave up holding onto her dress, a heavy orange extension cord emerging from her crotch area, snaking across the stage and disappearing into the sound booth. Barbra Streisand's "Jingle Bells" will never sound the same.

Every time she stepped on stage, it was anarchy. Lulu pulled me aside one day. "She's perfect. We need to adopt her." Ora became Tallulah's first daughter.

Then she landed a boyfriend who was a dress designer. How convenient. She had fresh gowns for every show. Her look shifted from anarchy to alluring: tall, thin, manicured, neat wig pulled back into a ponytail with a huge bow that always always always matched the dress, which was tailored, elegant, and simple.

She lost her first bid to be Empress. Her style was still too wild, too unpredictable. She was conquered in battle by an older Queen named Beverly Crest. Ora had to settle for second place in the palace for a year. That's when she became the mistress of court intrigue, blatantly manipulative, seductively scandalous, mysterious and mischievous. Princess Power Politics became her most important talent. She waited in the wings, watching and wanting and salivating. Everyone knew she would be the next ruler.

Beat.

Then along came Yoda.

I struggle for a moment to find a delicate manner of phrasing this next information, but graceful turns of tongue momentarily elude me.

Yoda was a little person. A tiny Queen.

Now for someone like Ora, for whom image equaled life, the remotest possibility of losing the crown she craved to — well — a vertically challenged person was unthinkable.

Yoda shopped in the junior petite section and did Anne Murray numbers. She was also becoming famous as dwarf tossing swept the bar scene. Yoda had the advantage of a novelty vote. How many other cities could successfully hold a circus-themed drag ball?

But Ora had waited for too long. Something had to be done. But what? A new proclamation? "Must be taller than this line to run for Empress"? In a secret meeting, the candidate committee ruled Yoda's application invalid.

Then, all hell broke loose.

Since word had gotten out, Yoda had garnered a lot more support than anyone had anticipated. Who could have known? Somehow the concept of a three-and-a-half-foot monarch didn't freak out the electorate. Lulu suddenly decided she was the Defender Of Dwarfs' Rights.

So Ora watched in horror as the ranks of Yoda's supporters swelled. People even defected to the other side once the movement started to pick up momentum. Ball weekend was approaching and the numbers were dangerously close.

The candidate committee finally caved to public pressure and allowed Yoda to run. Ora's performances began to feel a little desperate, like the stakes were getting higher. She had people coming from all over North America to witness her spectacular victory. She couldn't risk the sideshow. The public was now viewing her as the enemy in the Dwarfgate scandal.

Ora started to panic.

It was time to pull out the stops. Ora, in a last-ditch effort, returned to her roots: anarchy. She did the craziest things anyone had seen. New rumours started: Ora had been spotted on roller-skates being pulled by a station wagon down Fourth Street in a tutu in broad daylight; she rolled her mother's car and walked away from the wreck, laughing, and went back into the bar.

And the big finish: Police were called to a twenty-three-storey downtown high-rise known affectionately as Vaseline Towers — every city has one — to arrest a transvestite climbing the outside of the building balcony by balcony — in full glamour drag.

Opinion began to swing back. She was still the final word in glamour, but if it was a circus people wanted, she was only too willing to comply.

And somehow — it worked. She won by a landslide and was crowned Empress XII. The first words of her acceptance speech were "I'd like to thank the little people."

Maybe it was just people coming back to their senses, or maybe something in her reckless overdressed passion struck a chord in the rest of us. To see someone desire something so fiercely that she would risk life and lash to scale a downtown high-rise was an inspiring sight.

She stooped to conquer.

Ora's year as Empress marked the zenith of the glamour years in the Big Onion. She set a new standard for beaucoup de gownage, travelling extensively, wooing and wowing the circuit, living for the moment ... that shining, perfect moment ...

When Ora stepped down, the whole Hole Family was there. Lulu and I both did command performances, and I remember looking out from the stage and seeing what we had created ... since we had been crowned, every Mz. Flashback and every Entertainer of the Year and two of the Empresses had been descendants of Lulu and me, conceived in a flash of cosmic coincidence. In the snapshots from that evening, Lulu and I are surrounded by our beautiful, talented offspring. The photos speak as eloquently as any Rosetta Stone, preserving forever that time near the end of the millennium when lunacy met inspiration and a new spirit was born.

We were immortal now. All of us. Families go on forever.

Later that night, Ora broke up with her boyfriend, the dress designer, minutes after she crowned the next Empress. How convenient.

The Decline of a Drag Dynasty

The biggest challenge facing a monarch is knowing when to step aside. Longevity is a privilege granted to the Crowned Heads who rule their land with a velvet hammer. Most Royal Families eventually collapse under the sheer weight of their own self-importance. Revolution always starts in the palace.

Walla Walla West was falling apart. We lived in a warzone of eviction notices and disconnections, and money was scarce. Drag is an expensive drug. Trash left for Vancouver, leaving Lulu and I to take over Walla Walla West. Naturally, Trash left behind all of her stuff … after all, it was just garbage. Then Prickles took off to Europe ditching me with a twelve-hundred-dollar phone bill. Then Iona moved out to be with her sick mother. She made it just in time for the funeral. Finally, Lulu and I gave up. We had to; the kitchen wall fell in on Lulu as she did dishes. We left behind an eight-foot fig tree, a heavy metal sculpture, rooms full of drag, and the garbage from every Queen that had ever been there.

That house is gone now. So are a lot of the people who lived there.

Lulu and I moved into a walk-up on Jasper Avenue and then …

… and then I fell in love. And nothing can tear two sisters apart faster than a man.

I moved out while she was out of town. I never had the courage to tell her. Not to her face. We never talked about it. When we saw each other it was business as usual. But the damage had been done. We grew apart, even though we had pledged to stay together forever.

One day Lulu announced that she had landed a pro gig in Toronto with Rusty Ryan and the Great Imposters. I remember saying goodbye. I remember saying, "Pop a tuck, girl."

Lulu LaRude begat Gloria Hole begat Tallulah begat Ora Fice begat Mandy Kamp

The last year the Dynasty ruled was 1990. Mandy Kamp, Ora's Princess and eldest daughter, became Mz. Flashback 15.

She never stepped down. There was no Flashback by the time her year ended. The glass-brick wall was dismantled and moved out in the middle of the night. Pieces of it, and the rest of the club, ended up in garages and basements all over the city. An era of Edmonton's underground history was officially over.

By the time it happened, Lulu had already been in Toronto a couple of years. Just as well. She didn't have to watch our lives get hauled to the dumpster.

The Family, with no matriarch and no home, drifted across the globe and lost contact. With no escape from reality, we faced the light and started our new lives. We drifted like ice floes for a while, sometimes connecting, often missing ...

The club that ate Edmonton slipped away and sank under the water. We had all assumed she was unsinkable, that she would float forever, taking us on endless adventures.

Our lives, like lifeboats left after a disaster, seemed awfully small for a while. And lonely.

Happily Ever After

Isn't that how all fairy tales end?

This already feels like a lifetime away.

All I have to do is remember ... like I could ever forget.

What sounds like generations was over in less than one.

We came from all over Canada to land in the most unlikely of places.

We arrived in Edmonton with no family ... so we built one. We were fruitful. We multiplied. The generations blossomed and flourished and unfolded like ribbons of hope across the decade ... men stepping gracefully aside to give the Inner Woman free reign.

The world had ignored us, so we ignored the rules, creating a life of Pumps and Circumstance. Rather than hide our pain, we strapped it on and accessorized it. Wear your shame, girl ... and make it look better than God ever intended.

We became living, walking, breathing, screaming, chain-smoking art: a live canvas ready to be tweezed, shaved, waxed, plucked, painted, glued, beaded, teased, sprayed, and ultimately, displayed.

Then, like any piece of art, viewed, perused, mocked, scorned, criticized, adored, ignored ... Despite all the efforts to draw attention to ourselves, we became invisible.

The world ignored us when we started to disappear. At first, only we noticed.

Time became precious as real families reentered the drama, struggling to match the son they knew with the film noir movie star photos on the wall and the tiaras in the trophy case; a sudden desperate need to understand while it still mattered, while it could still make a difference.

The value of life skyrocketed.

I opened my piano bench one day and found a scrap of paper that had been in there since Walla Walla West ... it was one of Iona's poems, in her ballpoint scrawl:

Did I ever tell you

that when I was little,

I would stand under a streetlamp

and pretend that I was a beam of light?

When Iona died, she had already been in the Okanagan for a couple of years with her family. The last time she read her poetry in public, I could already tell she wasn't well.

I found out later that the night she died, we had all been talking about her at that exact same moment.

When Tallulah died, it had been two years since we had last spoken. We were never great about keeping in touch. When I heard the news, I put "I'll Be Seeing You" on the CD player, hit the repeat button, and sat for hours listening to the words that just weren't true anymore. Pieces of our last conversation floated back ... We had sat up all night, just like the old days. I made her tell me again about the moment when the eye surgeon peeled the bandages from her eyes and she saw the blue of his uniform, the first colour she had seen clearly in years. As the tears streamed down my face — 'cause that story had always chilled me — she stopped me short and asked me why I hadn't cried when she had told me that day in the drag room that she was dying.

I couldn't answer her. I didn't know how to cry back then.

When Ora died, I got the message on my answering machine. She had been hovering near death for a few days when they found her on the living room floor. All her furniture was piled up against the door of the apartment.

Who knows what she was trying to keep out.

At Ora's funeral, I went outside afterwards for a smoke. There in the parking lot was a car with the trunk open. Some Queens clustered around — I saw a flash of glitter — a Queenly fragment, a beaded carcass. It was one of Ora's gowns, bequeathed from one daughter to another. Ora was what she wore. What she was disappeared into a bag and was deposited in the trunk of a car that drove away in the rain.

Six months later, I got to hold her in my hands. Ashes are kind of like gravel. We each got a white balloon, and after saying a few words, we let the balloons go.

Brilliant sunlight.

The white balloons float higher and higher and further and further until they disappear in a blur of tears, the fog of memory — like some sad, languid, beautiful dream that fades even as you try desperately to remember ...

Some stars burn so brightly they consume themselves.

I sat by the river and wondered when it would stop.

It didn't stop.

When Ginger Snot died ...

When Prickles died ...

When Lori St. John died ...

When Yoda died ...

When Zola died ...

When Reena died ...

When Mother Jean died ...

When Joeboy died ...

When Millie died ...

When Excretia died …

When Grandma Kerr died …

When Sticky Vicki died …

When Bianca Bang-Bang died …

When Floratron died …

When Kim Burly died …

When Beverly Crest died …

When Sabrina died …

When Tinoir died …

When Tina died …

A news camera caught up with Trash, building stone sculptures on English Bay in Vancouver. He hoisted rocks twice his size, free-balancing them into memorials to his friends; sculptures as temporary as the lives they represented. As usual, Trash rearranged the landscape until it suited his mood, taking no credit until forced to. Art for him was like breathing; it just happened while you lived.

Lulu ended up in Halifax. God help the east coast. She took the town by storm. Lulu captivated as she always had, presiding over the Atlantic like a Zen mother. She spawned new generations of Holes with a fertile abandon, creating rich family histories that, for the moment, bound together the Outcast Elite: the Lucky Ones who got to see it all. Under her great wings, the real world disappeared. It flowed out of her like a river.

In the beginning, there was Lulu.

Before Lulu died, I visited her in Halifax. Lulu was so excited — she had managed to get her hands on a piano. She had wanted to make it a surprise, but couldn't help herself and sent me a picture of it sitting in her living room, ready to be played.

Needless to say, moments after I got there she made me start playing. For days I played, as Lulu would putter around behind me, tidying, reading, or hot-glueing beads to the headdress for her next show. Gradually, the songs came back — the Kate, the Rickie, the Joni, the Babs — her memory was amazing as she requested practically every song I had played while we lived together. And in one of those shining perfect moments when the sun is streaming in the window, I am transported back in time. I hear Lulu humming behind me. I finish the song. The ringing of the piano hangs in the air. "I love that song," she says. "I know," I say. And we are nineteen again. And the whole history of the world lies before us again. All the possibilities, the laughter, the heartbreak — all of it is just beginning again.

I remember what it was like to feel the magic that hovered between us. And never being afraid

Today, I look out my window at the river — my river — frozen, still and ghostly in the winter snow.

Years earlier I had stood on the High Level Bridge and opened the last of Ora's ashes. She scattered on the wind, falling into the river, disappearing into the murky flow. The water was brown, not blue. It's the same river, but older. It carries more within itself.

Time to start over.

My girls ... they knew how to live.

Then they learned how to die ... robbed of years of majesty, decades of potential.

Most of them didn't reach thirty.

It's easy to forget that all of these people lived with male names ... we were all "she" back then. I still call them that ... out of respect. For the art they created ... embodied.

So here's to us. To the Queens! We came from farms and cities and fishing villages and oil rig towns and dysfunctional families and well-adjusted families and minister's families. We are your hairdressers, your bank tellers, your mailmen, your teachers, your brothers, your sons, that hot guy that moved in next door ...

All we had in common was an age-old awareness that somehow we were different at the very core.

This isn't about not being good at hockey. It's about knowing from the word go that in a world of men and women, you are neither.

And both.

We are all born naked. Everything you put on after that is drag.

Their names are all now legend underground. The land they ruled over churns on and on without them. You can't stop time. Crowns get passed around like rhinestone cookie cutters; prizes for being the most ... whatever it is at the moment.

But here on earth, there's just big empty spaces where they used to be.

Every time I hear one of their old drag numbers, my favourite snapshot pops into view ... sculpted hair, lips quivering, arms stretched out at the standup mike, the brilliant spotlight cascading down then breaking like a million mirrors, refracted by jewels into shattering beams until we were blinded, their eyes gazing upward, sparkling with life and emotion and passion for their separateness, their existence, that moment ... like their entire life culminated on that stage in that moment, that shining, perfect moment ...

... the applause...

... the Lucky Ones.

Everybody should feel that before they die.

Slow fade to black.

THE EMPRESS

&

THE PRIME MINISTER

For Mr. ted northe, who dared to imagine a future Canada.

Thank you to the Alberta Foundation for the Arts.

BRADLEY MOSS

Artistic Director, Theatre Network

I HAVE been fortunate to work with Darrin Hagen on many productions as writer, actor, and sound designer. We first collaborated at the Edmonton Fringe on the 1999 Guys In Disguise production of *Pile-Driver!*, inspired by the true story of Canadian gay wrestler Harvey Jones. Later we remounted the production and toured it to Toronto's Buddies in Bad Times, where real wrestlers showed up to perform in our ring!

I have worked with Darrin on many of his plays: *Buddy*, where we used live cameras on stage and examined male toxicity and bullying; and the 2017 remount of his trailer park homage *Tornado Magnet*. I have also programmed many of his plays at Theatre Network, beginning with the earliest productions of *With Bells On*, and then fifteen years later, the adaptation *With Bells On: The Musical*. Our theatre lives have been intertwined for decades.

I owe Darrin a huge debt of gratitude for sharing with me his story and the stories of many Queer folks who have had to overcome outright judgement for just being alive. As artistic director of Theatre Network I have always valued plays that tell the story of how we can overcome difficult moments in our lives and create hope for the generations that follow us, how one individual can bring about change in others by standing firm in their right to be who they are and challenging those who think we all need to be the same.

As Darrin and I collaborated we would always make plans about what was next. We went through several phases, including a Michel

Tremblay phase, staging *La Duchess de Langeais* and then *Hosanna* almost back to back. And it was during this era — as part of the research for Hosanna's night of glory gone wrong — that Darrin introduced me to a drag ball where Queens were competing for the top prize of Empress. I had never been to a drag ball before; that night, Sticky Vicki was crowned as the new Empress "because she had her teeth done" (so they said). During the evening's acts there were breaks when everyone was stuffed together by the fire escape, smoking. As a young straight man and being new to scene of the Queens, I was now the outsider, the other, and I was royally teased with their quick cutting humour, shade, and innuendo. I quickly witnessed the drag queen's most powerful weapon: say it first, say it loud, and don't hesitate to shock. What fun I had being their foil that evening.

When Darrin approached me with his idea to create *The Empress & The Prime Minister*, the story of drag activist Mr. ted northe, he had just been witness to ted's speech at the Q Hall of Fame ceremony. Darrin spoke of blending northe's personal memoirs into a potent mix of passion, power, and politics. This self-styled Empress of Canada effected change in Canada, and his activism prompted Prime Minister Pierre Trudeau to champion the cause; the phrase "There's no place for the state in the bedrooms of the nation" caught fire in the media and the national imagination, leading to the partial decriminalization of homosexuality in June 1969.

Even though they were born decades apart, so much of Mr. northe's story is also Darrin's story as a drag queen, as a gender warrior, and as an activist. I immediately knew who we needed to cast as Pierre Trudeau: Joey L'Esperance was an actor I had worked with years before and I knew he would be the perfect choice to bring Trudeau alive onstage in both official languages (and to perform a knockout drag number!).

It's ted's story, but Darrin's lived experience permeates so many moments. When the character speaks of standing on the steps of the Courthouse in downtown Vancouver in full drag in 1958, Darrin's words speak to his own public life as a Queen — the vulnerability of speaking a new truth and the courage to step into the sunlight and reveal yourself. Those are Darrin's words, even as they must have matched ted's own experience.

I saw the very first production of *The Edmonton Queen*, during the holdover at our Roxy Venue. The end of that play hits hard: the audience slowly realizes that all of the photos scattered on the ground are of real people, Queens and friends destroyed by AIDS, an entire community devastated.

It is very fitting that these three plays featuring these Queens are published as companion pieces, as they represent Darrin's ability to convey his writing powerfully through performance. His work is compassionate, political, and distinct within the Alberta theatre view. Merged with his intense research is his own life, his vision of our society — from his unique outsider view — observant and sometimes critical, but always inspired by a thoughtful regard for the conflicted world he emerged from. And like Michel Tremblay, his plays resonate with audiences across the spectrum, because both writers draw upon the world around them with authenticity.

These three plays celebrate Darrin Hagen's career and — lucky for all of us — they can now be shared nationally and internationally. I am honoured to have played a role in all of them and to have witnessed Darrin Hagen's work as a drag performer/icon of Edmonton's underground (I first saw Darrin as a mermaid at Edmonton's Street Performers Festival) to his award-winning writing/performing as he champions the histories of sexual minorities — even as he himself was swimming against the tide of political or popular opinion.

Remember three things when you wave your hands: love my ceilings, love my drapes, and love my carpets!

CHARACTERS

Mr. ted northe*, self-proclaimed Empress of Canada

Pierre Trudeau, Prime Minister of Canada

Mama Jose (The Widow Norton)

Auntie Mame (The Rose Queen)

The Monsignor

Both actors play myriad federal politicians and media types

** Note: ted northe spelled his name without capitals in life; we have retained this style to honour his choice.*

Image courtesy of Ian Jackson / EPIC Photography; used with permission

PRODUCTION HISTORY

First produced by Theatre Network, Edmonton, Alberta, April–May 2019

Starring Darrin Hagen and Joey L'Esperance
Directed by Bradley Moss
Translation by Gisèle Villeneuve
Translation voiceovers by Cat Walsh
Set design by Scott Peters and Tessa Stamp
Lighting design by Scott Peters
Costume design by Tessa Stamp
Sound design by Darrin Hagen
Elizabeth Sterling Haynes Award Nominee: Outstanding New Play

Image courtesy of Ian Jackson / EPIC Photography; used with permission

Music. The Empress steps onto the stage and performs a lively drag number, complete with stuffed birds that she keeps tossing into the air, only to have them plop to the ground. During the final verse, snow falls from the sky. She bows, then heads to her drag mirror and sits and surveys herself.

ted: I have conjured this for you. All of this. Well — for me, really, but here you all are. Actually, I'm not really here. Because — well, I'm in a different place now. I'm channelling my story through this epic Queen you see before you. Or at least, that's how she describes herself.

But this Queen was willing. For the record, she doesn't look remotely like me. I did meet her decades ago when she was just a newborn princess, and she's managed to stay relevant. Not easy for a middle-aged crossdresser — I know that from experience.

Throughout history, men have dressed as women. It's a signal that a revolution is underway.

You've probably read the stories where men stormed the castle — there's always that quote that "some of the men were dressed as women." You thought, "Oh, I guess they were afraid to show their faces" or "What a strange disguise to choose." Or you may have thought, as I once did, "That can't be very practical, storming the castle in petticoats and wigs." I would picture an angry mob with torches — back then they were called faggots — the torches, not the mobs — I always imagined an angry faggot-bearing mob would be very hard on wigs — accidental fires on heads, hither and yon ... But in fact, they didn't dress as women to hide — they dressed as women because crossdressing is the uniform of upheaval, of radical change. An act of revolution.

Joan of Arc dressed as a man to lead her revolution ... but when the revolt was over, she didn't go back to dressing like a girl. She found freedom in the clothing of the revolution. And so, for practical reasons — practical reasons like fending off attempts at rape — while imprisoned, she was keeping her hair short ... and wearing pants.

She was burned at the stake for refusing to go back to wearing dresses; because of a biblical clothing law:

Deuteronomy 22:5. "A woman must not wear men's clothing, nor a man wear women's clothing, for the Lord your God detests anyone who does this."

Surely God had more important things to be concerned with.

Now. What have we learned from this story? When a woman puts on pants, she's unstoppable. Thus it follows that a man in a dress could also change the world.

The Empress begins to remove the dress and wig.

It seems fitting then — fitting — that I should be standing here now. In this dress. Years ago I stepped over the line. On the other side of the line lies the future that as of now I can only imagine. But on this side of the line I am just a faggot who should hang his head in shame. And while, yes, I am one — and have no intention of changing that — I *am* going to change the shame part.

It's almost our anniversary. All of us. And so I cast this spell.

Vancouver: 1966.

Vancouver. A dingy makeshift office/drag room. Dresses and wigs are everywhere. Protest signs lean up against the wall. ted is removing his makeup. Sound of a shop bell. Pierre enters.

PIERRE: Good afternoon.

ted: About time you got here. Sorry — I'm not ready.

PIERRE: Not to worry.

ted: You can help. There's pamphlets to pack up. I just finished printing them. That's what the smell is. Someone needs to invent an easier way of doing this.

PIERRE: I'm —

ted: A bit late, yes. I won't tell anyone. At least you showed up, unlike the rest of the fruits that said they would help me today. Can you grab these?

PIERRE: I can.

ted: We need to tidy this place up. He's going to be here any minute.

PIERRE: Who?

ted: Are you daft? The Minister of Justice is dropping in to see —

PIERRE: Should I have called first?

ted: (*finally out of his makeup so he can open his eyes*) Oh. My. You're him.

PIERRE: Good to meet you.

ted: I had no idea — so sorry — it's just that I'm all alone here today — activists can be such flakes ... Twelve people volunteered, but here I am, alone — well, not alone anymore, of course.

PIERRE: Take a breath.

ted: (*curtsies*) Your Highness.

PIERRE: I'm not sure that's the proper honorific.

ted: It's the only one I know.

PIERRE: It's good to finally meet you.

ted: I'd shake your hand but I'm covered in makeup remover.

PIERRE: So this is where the revolution is being planned.

ted: It's all we could manage.

PIERRE: It's charming.

ted: I can't believe you're here.

PIERRE: I'm glad to meet the man behind the letters.

ted: I send a lot of letters.

PIERRE: You made a compelling case.

ted: I make compelling cases all the time. But you're the first one who has listened.

PIERRE: You're a Liberal.

ted: What other choices do I have?

PIERRE: There are always choices.

ted: Choice is for people who are accepted.

PIERRE: That's all you want? Acceptance?

ted: Can I be honest?

PIERRE: Of course.

ted: I don't give a shit if people accept me or not. What I want is protection from the people that won't accept me.

PIERRE: You seem to have done quite well for yourself. Even without acceptance.

ted: I'm lucky.

PIERRE: How?

ted: My family. They're smarter than most. Plus, context is everything. I was nowhere as queer as my Uncle Bill. The dotty old fool. He would wait for men to open doors for him. No one really mentioned anything but everyone noticed. So whatever queer things my young mind was experiencing, they weren't as queer as Uncle Bill.

Dad always said that after all he saw in the military, nothing could faze him.

Plus we have enough money that we don't struggle. Of course, we aren't as rich as your family —

PIERRE: The money buys you the freedom to be an agitator. We have that in common.

ted: The money would mean nothing if my parents didn't accept me.

PIERRE: True.

ted: And we don't have *that* much money. But so many have so much less.

PIERRE: It's a cruel time.

ted: Especially for homos.

PIERRE: Are you comfortable using that word?

ted: I've been subjected to far worse. People like me have lots of words for people like me. But I'm too much of a Lady to speak most of them aloud around a man of such high standing.

PIERRE: Do you have words for men like me?

ted: Many.

PIERRE: What made you write to me?

ted: It's the only way to explain what needs to happen. You're not that special. I wrote to *everyone.*

PIERRE: The sheer number of letters — impressive.

ted: A man's life is at stake.

PIERRE: It sounds like you've created a real network in Vancouver.

ted: I'm sure you see the same out east.

PIERRE: Canada's a big country. There's a need for both.

ted: You should see how they organize south of the border.

PIERRE: Canada moves more ... tentatively than the States.

ted: It doesn't have to. It could lead the way. It should lead the way.

PIERRE: What makes you think the Liberal Party is the one to create the change you want?

ted: The Conservatives won't do it. The NDP would, but they'll never get elected. The Liberals are the first party to listen to me. Nobody listened. Until now. People like you don't usually stand up for people like us.

PIERRE: Politics is about timing. Being the right person at the right time. I have a feeling you know what that's like. I've been looking into many things since I entered the government. So many laws don't make any sense. A human being should have autonomy over the intimate details of their life.

ted: Pretty words. What happens when they accuse you of protecting child molesters? Because that's how some of them will paint us.

PIERRE: I grew up in a Quebec ruled by the Catholic Church. And when they lost their grip on power — prosperity. For me, it's proof that morality needs to be released from the grip of religion. A person's choices should be their own.

ted: If only.

PIERRE: Precedent. That's what makes me think it's time. Britain is moving in that direction.

ted: We're not England. England is so much more queer. And they know how to respect a Queen. That's how Uncle Bill got by with so little trouble. He taught in an English school. And it was an all-girl school. So nobody seemed to really recognize him as queer; him being English, he was very effeminate anyway — most of the English men are ...

PIERRE: Having the support of your family ... must make this easier.

ted: I realized that if I, with all of the good things that had happened in my life, with my family ... if *I* was having problems — then there were people out there that were having real problems. Much worse than mine.

So that was when I started studying and becoming involved and becoming an activist and questioning things ... I decided that I really needed to get my act together and learn about my government.

And about gayness. It was my homosexuality that I was most concerned about because that is the biggest part of my life. I don't have to worry about being a straight man and having children and "How am I gonna raise my children?" because that's not acceptable these days ... A gay man thinking about having a child ... Even *my* imagination has limits ...

Every person needs to decide what their life is for at some point. If you don't have a mission of some sort, what is life?

So I decided that I would have to start gearing all of my activities towards being a good queer. A good *Canadian* queer.

PIERRE: And so — are you?

ted: Darling. I'm the best queer. You'll see.

PIERRE: This is a long shot, you realize.

ted: You said there is precedent.

PIERRE: The Wolfenden Report.

ted: That was a decade ago. Across an ocean. It changed nothing here.

PIERRE: They've finally moved forward on its recommendations.

ted: In England.

PIERRE: What happens there affects us. We can do something similar here.

ted: Am I going to have to wait a decade for anything to happen?

PIERRE: No. I want to address it in the next parliament.

ted: You're going to stake your new posting on this?

PIERRE: Not exactly. It'll be an omnibus bill.

ted: What the hell does that mean?

PIERRE: The bill will include a myriad of policy changes, updates, revisions … the provisions concerning gross indecency will be just one part of it.

ted: Sounds sneaky.

PIERRE: They can't vote against it without also voting against the changes around divorce, contraception, impaired driving —

ted: It is sneaky.

PIERRE: It's time Canada had the conversation. Even the Church of England —

ted: Christ — I'm a patient Queen, but if I have to wait for the church to move forward we may as well give up.

PIERRE: Churches have influence.

ted: I don't go for churches. I had a bad experience.

PIERRE: When a church changes, it's significant. They're not known for their ability to adapt. Galileo.

ted: Joan of Arc. (*pause*) You're a practising Roman Catholic, aren't you?

PIERRE: In Quebec, it goes with the territory. I've managed to make it work for me. And you're …?

ted: A practising homosexual. Practice makes perfect.

PIERRE: But where do you find enlightenment?

ted: Must be nice to have the luxury of pondering existence.

PIERRE: Where do your parents go to church?

ted: Well, Grandma was Jewish. But that doesn't make me Jewish by default. I have faith in my own tenacity. But I worship nothing.

PIERRE: Non-practising Jew then.

ted: No. Not non-practising. I'm queer. I have no religion.

PIERRE: It isn't just about beliefs. Religion says much about how you were raised.

ted: So does being queer.

PIERRE: It has cultural implications. Community.

ted: So does being queer. It's more important to who I am than what church you attend is to you.

PIERRE: I doubt that.

ted: You can leave the church. I can't just leave queer behind. How can you be a practising Catholic and support queers? And divorce? And abortion? And contraceptives?

PIERRE: Religion is a personal relationship with whatever higher power you believe in. It should never override the law.

ted: That's new.

PIERRE: Is it?

ted: It is. Obviously you aren't running again ... because this is probably the last thing you'll ever do.

PIERRE: Why would I lose?

ted: You may be a little ahead of your time.

PIERRE: Then we have that in common as well. It's a matter of reason and law.

And it's time.

ted: Easy to say. (*looks Pierre up and down*) My first relationship was with a Catholic.

PIERRE: A Catholic boy?

ted: He wasn't a boy. But I was.

ted: I was never really part of a gay scene until I first went down to Los Angeles to study medicine. America was obsessed with the Cold War and the Red Scare ... and Marlon Brando was making outlaw bikers look very sexy ... The biker gangs back then were very different than what you see now ... then it was about horny young men living outdoors, in parks, on the road ... yes, they were having their fun. But in the cities, the community was beginning to gather in certain neighbourhoods, in certain taverns or hotels ... certain back alleys ...

I was interning at the hospital when a tall handsome *older* man entered. Some men carry an authority as they walk into a room. Now I know that it's *privilege* that allows a man to hold himself like that. But this man was queer too. How did I know? Well, I was quite the visual back then. Older men looked at me and they thought about fucking me. They couldn't help themselves.

And this man did that in the first three seconds. And he was certainly my kind of man. Regal. How does a queer access this kind of arrogance and confidence? It wasn't until later that I learned who he was ... and why he exuded power.

Duane was very well known in Los Angeles, where he was the Archbishop. Officially, the church didn't like gay people. Even the gays in the church didn't like gay people and I thought that was abhorrent.

But I learned so much from that man ...

Los Angeles, 1955

ted: I'm nervous.

MONSIGNOR: You'll like my friends.

ted: Are they all like you?

MONSIGNOR: That depends on what you mean by that.

ted: Handsome. Smart. Powerful.

MONSIGNOR: Let's just say they move in similar circles.

ted: Catholic?

MONSIGNOR: Most of them. But not all. The church allows me access to many levels of — influence.

ted: I'm excited. I've never been to the opera before.

MONSIGNOR: I think you'll appreciate the pageantry.

ted: Is that why you're in the church? The pageantry?

MONSIGNOR: It's not the most important reason.

ted: Tell me what happens in this opera.

MONSIGNOR: *La Bohème.*

ted: Okay. Sure.

MONSIGNOR: It's about destiny. And sacrifice.

ted: Sounds like church.

MONSIGNOR: It's about a conflict of cultures.

ted: Do you feel a conflict?

MONSIGNOR: Me?

ted: Being Catholic. And fucking me.

MONSIGNOR: Don't talk like that.

ted: Like what?

MONSIGNOR: I don't want you talking like that around my friends.

ted: You said yourself they're all queer.

MONSIGNOR: That's not how we do things. It's an understanding we all have.

ted: Not talking about it?

MONSIGNOR: We have positions to preserve. There's a manner in which to conduct yourself that will move you forward in life. Watch and learn.

ted: I'll be good. All the way through the third inning.

MONSIGNOR: Third act.

ted: But if you let me drink any wine, all bets are off.

MONSIGNOR: You won't need wine. Here. Smoke this.

ted: I'm not smoking grass before the opera. Do I look like a beatnik?

MONSIGNOR: It's not grass. Here. Try it.

The opium takes effect. The strains of a stunning aria. Suddenly they are in the opera audience. The music soars. ted watches Duane closely in wonder as Duane mouths the lyrics, gradually breaking down into sobs.

ted: Maybe it was the opium, but it was my first time in anything close to love.

But I was starting to realize how I fit into L.A.'s queer scene. The people I was meeting in the underground were the opposite of him: cruising defiantly, taking over parks, sharing new ideas, art, plans to change the world ... all happening right under the noses of the normal world.

I was looking at all these brave people and thinking "The whole world is opening up and — I'm in the middle of it!"

It was a very — a very free and a wonderful time for me — I thought it was the most exciting — you know, I just couldn't stand not being gay — you know, I just had to be as gay as I possibly could.

No wonder he was afraid of them. He had figured out how to move secretly through this world, and our generation threatened all of that.

MONSIGNOR: Where are you going?

ted: Out.

MONSIGNOR: Alone?

ted: Oh, I won't be alone.

MONSIGNOR: Stay.

ted: I need to see some people.

MONSIGNOR: Which people?

ted: I'll know when I meet them.

MONSIGNOR: I don't like you being out late by yourself.

ted: Lucky for you that I don't really plan to be by myself.

MONSIGNOR: You shouldn't be roaming out there at night.

ted: But that's the best time for roaming. Don't worry. I'll be careful.

MONSIGNOR: I do worry. There are predators.

ted: I'm a big boy.

MONSIGNOR: You don't know what's out there.

ted: Which is why I want to go out and see what's out there. Really, we could argue in circles all night. Or we could get to the part where you relent and I get what I want and everyone's happy.

MONSIGNOR: You should stay here.

ted: I've been studying hard. I need some fun. I want to try something new.

MONSIGNOR: I don't like —

ted: We seem to spend a lot of time talking about what you don't like. I want to spend time with my gay friends.

MONSIGNOR: You don't have any gay friends.

ted: I do. You just don't approve of them.

MONSIGNOR: We could invite someone over.

ted: Someone I choose?

MONSIGNOR: That wouldn't be safe.

ted: So *your* gay friends are fine. But mine aren't.

MONSIGNOR: It's for safety.

ted: I feel like I have already met all your friends.

MONSIGNOR: What have you got against my friends?

ted: Nothing. But they've all had me already.

MONSIGNOR: You speak like a whore.

ted: I've never mentioned getting paid. Is that an option?

MONSIGNOR: Listen to the way you talk. You're already soaking up the queers you meet.

ted: Unfortunate choice of words. But not entirely untrue.

MONSIGNOR: You need to be more careful. People talk.

ted: Let them talk. I'm not afraid.

MONSIGNOR: This flamboyant openness of yours is dangerous.

ted: I need some sort of outlet for it. Not everyone is lucky enough to wear a dress every day at work. What's the point in being surrounded by possibilities if I don't at least see what they are? I've never been one to hide. Not at home in Canada. Certainly not here.

MONSIGNOR: You're going to meet someone that will damage you.

ted: Far too late for that. I'm damaged by the world.

MONSIGNOR: I don't like who you associate with.

ted: Let me get this straight: as long as you choose who I fuck you're fine with me being a whore?

MONSIGNOR: I hate the way you talk.

ted: Is there anything you do like about me besides my ass?

MONSIGNOR: You act like a faggot.

ted: Oh my god, seriously? Have we met?

MONSIGNOR: I open my life to you —

ted: No you haven't!

MONSIGNOR: You're here aren't you?

ted: Yes. I'm here. But that's not enough for you apparently. Go ahead. Invite all your friends over. Tell them your whore is receiving visitors.

MONSIGNOR: Shut your filthy mouth.

ted: Come one, come all! And I mean that literally.

MONSIGNOR: Quiet!

ted: And why are your friends all safe but mine are all dangerous fags?

MONSIGNOR: Remember what happened last time you brought one of your friends into our circle —

ted: Come on, you know as well as I do that the confessional booth hides a multitude of sins. Some holy water, some absolution, and a dark booth with a strange sinner on the other side of the wall. That's not an evening in the church, darling. That's a night on the town. Hey — maybe that's where the fags got the idea! From you Catholics!

The Monsignor slaps ted hard across the face.

MONSIGNOR: You useless fag.

ted: How dare you.

MONSIGNOR: No. How dare *you*. Desecrating the concept of confession —

ted: Your closet is *your* problem, not mine. I have to go.

MONSIGNOR: Where?

ted: Someplace dark and smoky and full of real men.

MONSIGNOR: No. People will start to connect you to me. You don't want to be 'known' in this city.

ted: That sounds more like you.

MONSIGNOR: I'm sorry.

ted: No, you're not.

MONSIGNOR: I am.

ted: You say it so often, you can't possibly mean it.

MONSIGNOR: Please forgive me.

ted: I'm not God. I'm not letting you off that easy.

ted: He couldn't make me obey, and that pissed him off. He got worse and worse ... I knew it was over the day he tried to run me over with his car. Now I was in the hospital as a patient, not a nurse. That's when I realized what a dangerous place a hospital can be if you are different ... or powerless ... or queer ...

And that was when I got on the phone with my dad, and said, "I'm scared of this man — you need to come help me."

My father came and had a few words with the Monsignor. And took me back home to Canada.

I had thought I was in love ... and the fact that I had been rejected by him — because of my gayness ... and I thought, how many other people are out there that — you know, they don't have what I have — they don't have family, but they have somebody they've fallen in love with who's a real asshole ... or even worse, they have no one ... and they're dealing with it all alone ...

I thought it was my fault — because I wanted too much and I wanted to be a screaming fag — and I didn't realize that it was *his* problem. Not mine. He was so full of shame ... unable to control his impulses, and then spending hours a day trying to "pray the gay away."

When I came home I knew what kind of queer I wanted to be. None of this hiding inside the church. I wanted to empty my closet of fear and fill it with nothing but fabulous things. And so in Vancouver, I stepped into the light.

PIERRE: You challenged him. I challenge everything. It's in my nature.

ted: So how do you feel about faggots?

PIERRE: Are you trying to shock me?

ted: Well, I was. I'll stop.

PIERRE: My personal feelings are irrelevant.

ted: You're such a politician. Answer the question.

PIERRE: Well, for the record, I have a good deal of sympathy for the plight of the homosexual.

ted: Do tell.

PIERRE: And I know several.

ted: We are everywhere.

PIERRE: I know. I work with a few.

ted: Really? Who?

They both laugh.

ted: You don't have to tell me.

PIERRE: Good.

ted: But seriously, who?

PIERRE: Telling you their names would be dangerous.

ted: For them or for you?

PIERRE: Let's stick to politics.

ted: For my people, sex IS politics. George Klippert is in prison because of the politics of sex. For life. A murderer would get less time in jail.

PIERRE: Klippert is a brilliant opportunity. His case drives home the idea that the law needs to be changed.

ted: They weren't even after him. You know that, right? They were questioning him about an arson. And somehow figured out he had sex with men. And so they charged him. They didn't even have to catch him doing it. All they needed was an admission that it had happened in the past, and that he couldn't ever change it. This is the problem: if you're gay, you fear the law. You don't ever call the cops — not even if you need them. Because they may walk into your home, see a Barbra Streisand poster and toss you in jail.

PIERRE: You like Barbra Streisand?

ted: You're kidding right? Queens love Babs.

PIERRE: She's an interesting woman.

ted: She's magnificent. She doesn't fit in. She plays by her own rules. My people love a rebel. That's why I noticed you. It's rare to see a politician ready to take a stand. But politics punishes rebels.

PIERRE: Not always. (*pause*) You're not intimidated by me.

ted: My time with the Monsignor taught be not to be intimidated by power.
Should I be?

PIERRE: Some are. I don't suffer fools.

ted: Welcome to the Rebel's Club.

PIERRE: Rebels change the world. There's research being done. Kinsey —

ted: Yes, everyone's studying the pansies nowadays. I've seen it up close.

There used to be this odd flaming queer that lived in the West End. Outrageously nellie — we called her Mercy May, and when she would see a hot man on the street she would run up and grab his dick and cop a feel and run away screaming "Mercy! Mercy!" She was often attacked for this. She was beat within an inch of her life. But she wouldn't stop.

The talk around town hinted that Mercy May had met the fate of many homosexuals of that decade — he had been lobotomized in the mental hospital. This crazy wild creature running up and down Davie — that was all that was left of a once-normal beautiful gay man.

PIERRE: You mixed up 'he' and 'she'.

ted: No, I didn't. Pronouns become meaningless in this new world. Welcome to the future.

When I got back to Canada, I couldn't be a nurse in a regular hospital. They wouldn't hire a man. And so I found a place where my new skills could make a difference: in the mental homes.

It's the mental hospital where the real tragedies are. It's chemical castration. It's conversion therapy. Electroshock therapy. Trying to correct us when there's nothing wrong.

I've seen what they do to homosexuals that get in trouble. Klippert is one of the lucky ones. He went to prison.

They're not studying us. They're torturing us.

PIERRE: You don't seem to think any of this is possible.

ted: I don't.

PIERRE: Then why try at all?

ted: Because —

... because ... I have to do something. I swore an oath.

PIERRE: Then let's do something. Together. Now you have access to power.

ted: Oh, I've had access to power before. The Archbishop. The Premier.

PIERRE: Which premier?

ted: You're not my first politician. I looked after two of Premier Manning's sons in Alberta. Including the one no one talks about, because he had to be "hidden" from view — because of the shame of having a child who was less than normal in a world that was all about appearances. I cared for those boys for years. So I have seen up close how politicians work. Promises can change when they become liabilities. People can be hidden away when they become a challenge to an agenda.

I've raised my issues with many powerful men. I'm used to being turned down or mocked. You're the only one who responded.

PIERRE: But I'm the right one to respond. Every letter stands for a dozen people who think like you do, but are afraid to say it. Have you read the editorials? The media is outraged by the Klippert decision. Not one of them feel this is just. They don't feel hate, they feel pity —

ted: We don't need pity.

PIERRE: Take what they offer. They have influence. And your letters — they're being read. And the timing — can you feel the change happening?

ted: That's all academic. In the real world, queer life is still brutal.

PIERRE: Your passion makes you care. But your reason is what will make you effective. See the change happening. And then figure out how to exploit it.

ted: I don't see enough change.

PIERRE: You are the change!

I've been following the battle. The police are wasting their time.

ted: You'd never know it from the amount of times we are arrested.

PIERRE: They've tried everything. They tried to map all the places in Ottawa where men gathered. They put a red pin in a map of the city every time they arrested a homosexual. Within weeks the map was a sea of red dots.

ted: We know how to paint the town red.

PIERRE: So now the police have moved on to a new tactic.

Deep inside a police station. a doctor is attaching a policeman to a machine.

COP: So ... what exactly does this thing do?

DOCTOR: It measures responses. It rates stress levels.

COP: Is that all?

DOCTOR: Unbutton your shirt, please.

COP: What kind of responses?

DOCTOR: There's the pupillary response test. Another measuring your pulse.

COP: Responses to — what?

DOCTOR: Responses. To certain images.

COP: Like a Rorschach test?

DOCTOR: I suppose.

COP: Images of what? Puppies? Waterfalls?

DOCTOR: Not exactly. Can you lift your arm?

COP: There's a lot of rumours about these tests.

DOCTOR: Policemen deal with a lot of stress. We want to learn to measure and manage that stress.

COP: How come I'm the only one here?

DOCTOR: We're having trouble getting volunteers.

COP: No wonder. You know what they're calling this machine?

DOCTOR: It's not a machine. It's a test.

COP: They call it the Fruit Machine.

DOCTOR: That's unfortunate.

COP: Maybe this isn't such a good idea —

DOCTOR: You're helping the police in a significant way.

COP: I'm not a fag.

DOCTOR: No one is insinuating that you are.

COP: I mean, that's why I'm here, right? You need normal guys.

DOCTOR: It's called "the control" in a scientific experiment.

COP: "The control."

DOCTOR: After testing some normal men — "controls" — we will know how to spot anomalies and clues when we test suspected homosexuals. I'm just going to attach these here ...

COP: What kind of things are you measuring?

DOCTOR: Pupil dilation, heart rate ...

COP: Okay ...

DOCTOR: Blood flow to the penis —

COP: What?

DOCTOR: Please undo your pants.

COP: You're going to measure my boner?

DOCTOR: Are you going to get one?

COP: What?

DOCTOR: An erection.

COP: I'll be honest — maybe I'm not the right guy — I get hard pretty easy.

DOCTOR: I'll make a note of that. We don't — need to measure —

COP: Okay. So ... what are you gonna show me?

DOCTOR: Various photos.

COP: Like — porn?

DOCTOR: There will be some erotic images.

COP: Okay. I can do this.

DOCTOR: Now ... would you like to fasten this electrode to the base of your penis, or would you prefer that I do it?

COP: Are your hands cold?

DOCTOR: I'm afraid so.

COP: Then you'd better do it.

DOCTOR: As you wish. (*The examiner reaches toward the cop's crotch.*)

COP: You know what? I've changed my mind.

DOCTOR: But —

COP: Yeah, I gotta go. Good luck with your test.

DOCTOR: I'll have to make a note on your record.

COP: You do that, Doc.

ted: What a pointless waste of energy.

PIERRE: All of it is. For years their best source of rooting out homosexuals was to terrorize other homosexuals.

ted: You can stop saying 'homosexual.'

PIERRE: What term do you prefer?

ted: We're saying "gay" these days. It's the latest.

PIERRE: That doesn't seem like it will catch on.

ted: Why not?

PIERRE: It already means something else.

ted: So does faggot. And queer. And pansy. And fairy.

PIERRE: Touché.

ted: And fruit.

PIERRE: For a long time the police have relied on *your* people to find others like you. Once they arrest one, they use the threat of prison or having the secret revealed to gather names.

ted: I know this already. It's despicable. They take the little black books of the men they arrest. And they make a "Queer List." And then they call up every number looking for more. Then they call it a "ring" of perverts even though most of the men have never met each other.

PIERRE: What you may not know is that the men they arrest — well, lately, something interesting is happening.

ted: Tell me.

PIERRE: Homosexuals —

ted: Gays.

PIERRE: — were always ready to name other homosexuals—

ted: Gays. Trust me, it gets easier.

PIERRE: — to protect themselves. But now — gays —

ted: Good for you. See? New terminology can be hard. It takes time.

PIERRE: — stay silent.

ted: Really?

PIERRE: You're surprised?

ted: Well — I've never given over any names. I've always hoped we would stop turning each other in. I just never pictured it happening.

PIERRE: It's happening. I have sources.
So ... Have you ever been arrested?

ted: I'm queer. So ...

PIERRE: You did something illegal?

ted: My whole life is illegal. I break the law as soon as I open my eyes.

PIERRE: Let's change the law.

ted: You make it sound like it's going to be easy.

PIERRE: It won't be easy.

ted: So what does this mean? What do you need me to do?

PIERRE: Organize. Rally your community.

ted: Petitions? Pamphlets?

PIERRE: Oh, it will be lots of that.

ted: Persuasion?

PIERRE: Even more important.

ted: You think Canada is ready.

PIERRE: I know that *I'm* ready. And I have a feeling *you* have been ready for a long time.

ted: Revolution. It's finally here. Now I need to figure out what to wear.

ted rushes to the rack of dresses and starts holding them up one at a time to see which ones look best.

PIERRE: Remind me what tonight is.

ted: It's a drag show. Everyone will be there. It's the perfect moment to get a whole bunch of people on our side all at once.

PIERRE: Do I need to say anything?

ted: I know how to talk to them. You just stand there and wave and look French.

PIERRE: It doesn't seem like very practical uniform for revolution.

ted: Then you have never seen a drag queen fight. A high heel is a dangerous weapon.

PIERRE: Tell me something.

ted: Anything.

PIERRE: Why do you dress like a woman?

ted: Seriously? Sash, crown sceptre, gown — I dress like a *monarch*. There is a difference. How many women do you know that dress like this?

PIERRE: Only the Queen.

ted: Exactly.

PIERRE: She's a woman.

ted: She's also an idea. Personified in female form.

PIERRE: So you don't want to be a woman?

ted: I don't need to be a woman. I already know what it's like to be treated like a second-class citizen.

PIERRE: How does dressing as a Queen change all of that?

ted: Because then I am the concept personified. People need to hear our message. They won't listen to a young rural boy, a faggot with zero clout. But they will listen to Mr. ted northe: Man In A Dress! Once they stop staring, of course.

PIERRE: So you dress — like — this — and then you perform?

ted: Actually, I tend to wear this more for protesting than for performing. It makes me harder to ignore. But tonight, I'll be performing. Trust me. All I have to do is leave the house dressed like this and it's a show.

PIERRE: What kind of performance?

ted: Have you never seen a drag show?

PIERRE: No.

ted: So privileged and yet so deprived.

Most drag queens lip-synch. Trust me, it's for the benefit of everyone. There are queens who use their own voice, but they are few and far between. I do like that new girl on Singalong Jubilee. I hope she does an album. Anne Murray, that's her name.

PIERRE: Do you sound like her?

ted: This baritone was created for screaming, not singing.

PIERRE: Would you try and look like Anne Murray?

ted: Please. I'm far too feminine.

PIERRE: Please don't take this the wrong way — it seems ... a tad frivolous.

ted: You're new to this so I'll cut you some slack. I had no choice.

PIERRE: But if you don't want to be a woman —

ted: All I know is that I have always felt like I am more than one human. The one that people see — and the one they can't. Maybe because queers are so used to hiding their true selves — we only show the part of us that's safe. Maybe because I was a twin, I've always felt like I'm two people. In one person. I needed to follow that impulse.

PIERRE: You have a twin?

ted: Had. It was a complicated birth. My parents were on vacation in Cooking Lake when Mom went into labour. He only lived a few hours.

Maybe I'm trying to give him a voice. Maybe he's the missing part of me. As a Queen I can explore that.

PIERRE: Maybe I should call *you* Your Majesty.

ted: I would adore that.

PIERRE: Where does one learn this — craft?

ted: I prefer the term "art form." But there's no school. You gotta go to the source. Now — could you put all of this in my closet?

PIERRE: Back in the closet you go ...

ted: I first spotted it when I travelled to San Francisco. I loved what I saw there, even as baffling as it was.

I watched men embrace their inner divas — and unleash them in a flamboyant display of faggotry. It flaunted disrepute and at the same time, demanded legitimacy.

Defiance. Courage. And balls ... dressed in gold lame and feathers and rouge and liquid liner and silver strap-ons. It was gaudy, garish, grotesque, and it didn't give a fuck what anyone thought. It was everything it had to be. And it happened in the smoky dirty grubby bars and cafes and darkrooms.

I had heard of this bar — they never dared to call them gay bars back then, but everyone knew who gathered there. The bohemians. The outcasts. People like me.

And so I decided to visit this bar — The Black Cat.

San Francisco 1956. Pianoman sits at a piano, sings a Black Cat welcome song. Sounds of a seedy lounge and an appreciative audience.

PIANOMAN: (*sung*) *Hello hello everybody*
I'm glad to see you are here
To sing and dance and
Entertain you
And bring your lives a cheer
For all of us are a dandy
On that of course you can rely
So hello hello everybody
We all welcome you
The Black Cat welcomes you
We are glad that you're here!

Ladies and gentlemen and everyone in between — that's most of you — now is the moment you have all been waiting for. The Black Cat is thrilled to present to you, the Diva of the Downtrodden, the Goddess of Glamour, the Cantatrice of The Resistance, the Prima Donna of the Tenderloin District, the Queen of All the Americas: The Widow Norton herself, the legendary Mama Jose!

Mama Jose steps into the spotlight.

MAMA: And I know why you're here … for some culture, right? For a taste of how the upper classes spend their time. A little opera for you all? Yes? Yes! Everyone said yes — except for you. Yes, you. Hello, sailor. First time off the ship? I'll go easy on you. Now pay attention, you handsome man. This is very sophisticated stuff. You should learn this. You won't always be beautiful, you know. You'll need something to talk about when the plumbing gets rusted. Yes, I'm talking to you ….

She performs an aria from Carmen *in full falsetto. Applause. She retreats to her dressing room. ted knocks on the door.*

JOSE: *Entrar*! (*pause*) Come in!

ted: Wow. You were magnificent.

JOSE: Hey kid. Where are you from?

ted: Vancouver.

JOSE: Way up north? *Bonjour, mon ami*!

ted: I'm sorry — I don't —

JOSE: But you're Canadian.

ted: Lots of us don't speak French. I'm impressed that you do.

JOSE: You come from a bilingual country and can't speak one of its languages? I come from a place where they can barely speak English and I speak four languages.

ted: Four?

JOSE: I was a translator in the army. Eventually the military decided that me being gay overshadowed my gifts. But I showed them. I said to myself, "You sons of bitches! Fine! You named me a homosexual ... You label me a Queen? Then I'll be the best goddamn Queen that ever was!" Sons of bitches.

What brings you all the way down here?

ted: I've been a regular ever since I came to California to study.

JOSE: Where does one study to be queer? I could teach!

ted: No. To be a nurse.

JOSE: Ah. They don't have that up in Canada.

ted: Actually they do.

JOSE: Really? Amongst the igloos?

ted: Umm — Vancouver is a big city.

JOSE: Sure, sweetie.

ted: You should come visit someday.

JOSE: I should. I hardly ever get to wear my fur coats here.

ted: You have more than one?

JOSE: Of course. One for wearing and one for dragging. I have never been north of Portland. My sister Auntie Mame holds court there.

ted: Auntie Mame? Is she like you?

JOSE: Nowhere near as good of a singer. Bad teacher. But a grand Queen nonetheless. You want to see something grand? You should go to Portland. Twice a year they crown a new Rose Queen.

ted: What's it like? To perform dressed like that?

JOSE: Like what? Oh! You mean this. Well, you have no business on a stage unless you dress the part. Ever been onstage?

ted: I'm a dancer. An Arthur Murray instructor.

JOSE: Ahh, the refuge of the man who's light in the loafers. I thought you were a nurse.

ted: I'm both.

JOSE: Proving once and for all you CAN do everything — you just can't do everything at once.

ted: They really love you.

JOSE: They do. I'm their goddess.

ted: Is this your bar?

JOSE: Take that back. I know I fit right in like a piece of old furniture darling, but I'm not that old. This nasty dive has been here since 1908. But it might as well be mine. Every nasty sticky smelly square foot of it, darling. Do they have sophisticated bars like this up in the tundra?

ted: We have the same climate as you —

JOSE: Sure you do.

ted: Canada's not that different. But we don't have bars like this. There are bottle clubs ... places to meet where you bring your own booze ... sometimes it's in someone's living room. You can sometimes find your own people in the straight bars. They separate the single men from the women with dates. So, it could be very easy to go into the "males only" part of the bar and find somebody that was looking for some action just by looking around.

But we have to be more careful up north. Not like here.

JOSE: Trust me, we have to be careful here too. The cops still come through all the time. I've been arrested more times than I can count. One of their favourite ways to harass the queers is to arrest all the drag queens.

ted: What law are they breaking?

JOSE: Dressing as a woman "with the intent to deceive." It meant that as soon as the cops raid a bar or gathering, every drag queen in the place is forced to remove her wig. To prove she's not "intending to deceive."

ted: That's horrible.

JOSE: I know. All that work and hairspray, down the drain. And so I made a whole bunch of black patches in the shape of a cat's head. And then I stitched the words I AM A BOY. That way, there's no way they can claim we're trying to fool or trick anyone. Here — have one.

ted: But I don't do drag.

JOSE: Not yet. But a ballroom-dancing nurse? You're already halfway there.

Trust me. I have an eye for these things. Welcome to the counterculture. The resistance.

There's nothing wrong with being gay — the crime is getting caught. That's why we all need to stick together. United we stand, divided they catch us one by one. Sons of bitches.

ted: It had never occurred to me to dress in drag, even though I did have a craving for applause. Ballroom dancing had me competing in cities up and down the west coast, from Vancouver to San Fran and all points in between. I paired with a marvellous young lady whose last name was Winters. They called us Northe & Winters.

I loved every new city I visited, because that meant seeing how queers in other cities existed. Sometimes you could find thriving little cadres in the most unlikely places. Eventually I took Mama Jose's advice and landed in Portland, Oregon: the last place one would expect to find a society of queers that had created their own world.

Auntie Mame was presiding over an empire that was rapidly becoming a force to be reckoned with. One spring I arrived in town just in time for the crowning of the new Rose Queen.

Portland's annual Rose Queen Coronation, 1957. ted and Mame enter, applause and music ringing out from behind them. Mame is in full high drag.

MAME: Have you ever seen hundreds of queers all dressed to the nines in full royal regalia before?

ted: Never.

MAME: It's an inspiring sight, isn't it? My people.

ted: So is this a costume contest or a pageant?

MAME: It's both. And yet it's so much more than that. It's a Coronation. And it's about eight hours long.

ted: How does a man dressed like that change the world?

MAME: However the fuck she wants. It's more likely to work than what I did before this.

ted: What did you do before this?

MAME: Military.

ted: Wow. What is it about all you military guys that end up being drag queens?

MAME: I think it has something to do with nature trying to rebalance herself after overexposure to testosterone. You'll be singing a different tune once you try it.

ted: I want to try it. But I don't know what to do.

MAME: Live it large. Live it loud. Just live it, darling.

ted: Like this?

MAME: God no. Not like that. First you need to find a song that gives you goosebumps. Or makes you laugh.

ted: What do you suggest?

MAME: I'm not giving you any of my songs! You need to find your own. Start listening to anything with a female singer.

ted: Does it have to be a female singer?

MAME: Well, it won't make much sense otherwise.

ted: But — I don't want to pretend to be a woman ...

MAME: Trust me — no one will think that. But if you want to reinvent the wheel, be my guest.

ted: Mama Jose said —

MAME: Ahh yes, Mama Jose. You understood her? Good for you. Speaks four languages — none of them right. I taught her everything she knows.

Unfortunately I didn't teach her everything *I* know ...

ted: She can sing. But I can dance.

MAME: Good. So you'll need a few classic drag moves. Oh, and — I'll teach you how to pirouette.

ted: When will I ever use a pirouette?

MAME: You just never know when it may come in handy. Fleeing from the police, for instance. No reason not to do *that* in style ...

They move to the makeup mirror and Mame begins to transform ted into a Queen.

ted: Why do the police always arrest drag queens?

MAME: Darling, we're the low-hanging fruit. They arrest us because they want us to go back to hiding in shame. So the best way to steal that victory from them is to shed the shame.

The gay nation needs leaders. And we are the most visible. Otherwise we have no figureheads. No heroes. No politicians. That means we have no representation. Our most potent weapon is our numbers. And so they try to keep us from gathering.

They say we are bad for their community. So we create our own community. And then WE can decide what the rules, the morals are.

The Rose Coronation gets bigger and bigger every year, and more and more men want to become the Rose Queen.

Drop the shame. Play the game.

Things are changing. But it's slow. It's going to take all of us working together. My sisters.

ted: What if you get arrested?

MAME: They can't break me. They seem to forget that I've had my whole life to figure out how to be happy in this fucked-up world.

The queenly transformation continues as ted speaks.

ted: She was actually Joan of Arc. Auntie Mame helped created the Imperial Rose Empire. Soon, she and Mama Jose had established a monarchist society. But they wanted to call themselves Queens and I resisted. Canada already had a queen. Americans don't really understand the distinction, but when I suggested they call themselves Empress instead, they loved it. For a decade I travelled to attend as many of their events as I could ... and I soaked up the pageantry. And eventually I realized what role the Church must have played in the Monsignor's life. It was about belonging to something bigger than yourself. And the ritual. And the pageantry. And being around people who believed in the same thing you did.

I saw what they did. I was as surprised as anyone that it worked. And so I vowed that I would do what they had done. I would bring that glamourous and epic battle to the frozen tundra of my childhood.

MAME: Tundra? Didn't you grow up in the Fraser Valley?

ted: Please — I'm in the middle of embellishing.

Transformation complete: a grand royal drag creation.

I decided that I could help by launching the same idea in Canada. In Vancouver. The whole west coast of North America would be one solid Queendom from north to south. It was the first time that men in drag reached out and held hands from city to city. None of us knew what would happen. What we did know was that *something* would happen.

You can't use that much aerosol hairspray without altering the world somehow. That's just a guess.

Auntie Mame and I decided that this new society transcended political borders. We were creating a nation of queers. With our own laws, and our own rituals — even our own national costume. Hey — maybe someday we could even have our own flag!

It was in Portland that Auntie Mame herself bestowed upon me the greatest honour I would ever receive — one that would change the way I saw the world forever. It was 1964, and my dear Sister-Queen crowned me Empress of Canada.

Music. Ecstatic cheering. Mame places the sceptre, sash, and finally the crown on ted's head.

I — Mr. ted northe — humbly accept the responsibility I have been entrusted with. I will fight for the dignity of my queer family and dedicate my life and my passion to the quest for equality. I pledge before you now that my entire life, my body, my soul, and my heart, now belong to the queer nation.

Applause. The Empress curtsies, gives a royal wave.

As the applause fades …

ted: It was a far cry from where I started.

Nine years earlier, I had taken a page from Auntie Mame's instructional guide to stirring the pot.

MAME: (*voiceover*) No one will listen to a queer — but no one can ignore a man in a dress.

Vancouver, 1958

ted: And so there came the day when I had to put that to the test. In full high drag, with all the grandeur I could manage at the age of twenty-one, I walked down Robson in my high heels, heading straight for the courthouse. It was full daylight. I was shaking. Never in my life had I actually crossed over that line — and what I was about to do would erase that line forever.

It was August 26, 1958. I remember that clearly, because I could feel the winds of change guiding me down the street.

Yes, people stared. But no one tried to stop me. And no one said a word.

I made my way up the staircase to the entrance of the courthouse. This gave me a stunning vantage point of Robson at rush hour. Highly visible but just out of reach.

What the fuck was I doing? I marvelled at the insanity of it all. I was a fool to do it alone. I know that now.

What I didn't realize about standing in the open, dressed like that, is how permanent it is. It comes off. But you can never remove it completely. It stains you. You need to embrace that, because it's never going away. The moment they see you — they know what you are.

I made my sign as big as I could make it. But it was silent. Easy to ignore. Those who noticed sneered and kept moving.

"I AM A HUMAN BEING!"

It was just a matter of time before the police arrived. They pulled my arms behind my back and slapped the cuffs on me. And when they asked me my name, I remembered what Auntie Mame had taught me.

MAME: (*voiceover*) Remember … you aren't impersonating a woman. You are a gay man in a dress.

ted: They asked me my name, and I responded in my most confident baritone: "*Mr. ted northe.*"

That was the first time I got my name in the papers. But not the last. Once I had been through it, I wasn't as scared … Sad that one could get accustomed to getting arrested, but it's true. The booking process even had some moments of hilarity. I was told female impersonation was a crime, and that I needed three items of male clothing or I would be tossed in a cell. I reached into my bra and pulled out two wool socks as masculine as any socks could be. Then I reached under my dress and pulled off my Fruit of the Looms and tossed them onto his desk. Easy as one, two, three.

I became a regular disturbance in downtown Vancouver. There was safety in numbers, so I assembled a gang that would protest with me. The media began referring to us as The Lavender Mob. We held the police accountable. Normally cops got away with abusing queers. Well, we stopped being ashamed. Soon we knew their names as well as they knew ours.

"Yoo hoo, Officer Jones! Wanna give me a ride down to the station?"

It became second nature to stand outside the notorious men's room at the downtown Eaton's with a sign warning all the potential cruisers that the police were regularly sweeping through, arresting anyone caught with a cock in their hand. Gay or not.

We started standing up for ourselves. In this new era, every faggot carried a small bag with them — a place to hold protection. So if you and a girlfriend were mincing gaily, like we sometimes did, and some ruffians take offence, like they sometimes did, and they attacked ... bear spray. Right in the fucking eyes.

Take advantage of their momentary blindness and confusion and kick them in the balls. Or take your purse with the heavy can of Sudden Beauty in it and smack them in the head. "I don't know what happened, Officer. He just ran into my purse. Face first. Eleven times." It isn't as cruel as baseball bats to the skull.

We *have* to stick up for ourselves. Because no one else will. And the thugs never call the police. No red-blooded Canadian man is gonna tell a cop that a fairy kicked the shit out of him.

When one faggot stands up and says 'no more', he stands for dozens that are hiding, trying to stay invisible.

ted removes the wig and headdress.

This faggot has nothing to lose. It has to change. The law has to change.

ted sits and starts removing his makeup.

Outside the House of Commons, Ottawa. Press scrum.

PIERRE: It's certainly the most extensive revision of the Criminal Code since the 1950s and, in terms of the subject matter it deals with, I feel that it has knocked down a lot of totems and overridden a lot of taboos and I feel that in that sense it is new. It's bringing the laws of the land up to contemporary society, I think. Take this thing on homosexuality. I think the view we take here is that there's no place for the state in the bedrooms of the nation ....

ted: *(still removing his makeup)* That phrase — a brilliant piece of wordplay. It shot across the airwaves like lightning. It was an undeniable stroke of genius. Only a great man would sum up the hypocrisies of the law so succinctly.

PIERRE: The truth is — I didn't come up with that line myself. I read it in a Globe and Mail article a few weeks earlier. And that writer lifted it from the Wolfenden Report.

ted: It didn't matter.

PIERRE: It's still a good quote. I can't help it if I said it best ...

REPORTER: *(voiceover)* And what if the bill fails?

PIERRE: I always feel that if you're on the Liberal side, you should ... take risks on the side of progress, and if you're going to be beaten you should be beaten because you've been too progressive.

ted: Pierre was the most quotable politician Canada had ever witnessed.

PIERRE: You scratch my back — I'll scratch yours. Don't scratch my back and I'll scratch your face.

ted: I once heard him say to an adversary:

PIERRE: I'll bury you.

ted: And he meant it.

REPORTER: *(voiceover)* Do you expect to run into any personal roadblocks in the House over the Homosexuality provisions?

PIERRE: (*howling with laughter*) I have had many homosexual friends in my life in both the artistic and intellectual communities. But I was never one myself.

ted: Now, I always thought he was very "gay" — by that I mean very, very demonstrative, and a hugger and a toucher. I mean, I used to have to fight to keep my hands off him. He was a sexy cocksucker. And he wore some really tight pants.

Because he had introduced the bill, there were rumours throughout the political sphere, especially in Quebec. One MP said the bill was for fairies and queers — "Oh and by the way, Trudeau is still a bachelor, hint hint ..."

When another MP confronted him in the House of Commons lobby and asked flat-out if Trudeau was queer —

PIERRE: Perhaps the men making these charges should leave me alone with their wives for a couple of hours.

ted: It was easy to feel like the world really was capable of seismic change, and not just of the volcanic sort. We had been led by old men. Many of us had had enough of that.

He was right. It was time. Against all odds, Pierre ran for — and won — the leadership race for the Liberal Party.

Thunderous cheering. Pierre addresses his party.

PIERRE: This is an extremely great honour that I have received from this great assembly of Liberals; an honour and a very heavy responsibility.

And the only way in which I can show appreciation for this honour will be to bear this responsibility with all my strength and with all my energy.

Canada must be unified. Canada must be one. Canada must be progressive and Canada must be a just society.

Still more thunderous applause. The sound fades slowly.

ted: And then he called an election. I was crushed. All pending legislation died. Including the only bill I had ever cared about. He said he was willing to campaign on these radical ideas. And reintroduce it once he won. But — what if he lost? What if Canada wasn't ready and rejected him?

And then something amazing happened: Trudeaumania. It's hard to explain if you weren't there to see it yourself — but the media treated him like a celebrity. I've seen hordes of young ladies screaming hysterically for a rock band before, but never a politician. This was all new. Maybe he was right — maybe Canada was ready. Suddenly, image mattered. Style mattered. And that bastard had style. And the cameras loved him.

I was thrilled to spend even a moment with him when the campaign wound its way back west to Vancouver. By now he was a star — the rest of the country was now realizing why I was so captivated by him. I had to fight through gaggles of young ladies to stand by him. I used to laugh because I remember acting like Queen Victoria, saying "Mr. Prime Minister!"

PIERRE: You shouldn't call me that.

ted: Why not?

PIERRE: I'm not prime minister yet.

ted: You will be if I have anything to say about it. I've taken care of everything. I've rallied the troops.

PIERRE: I appreciate your confidence.

ted: You're the most important man I've ever met, "Mr. Prime Minister!"

Pierre laughs mischievously.

That's the only time I ever hear you laugh — when I say "Mr. Prime Minister." Could I ask you a question? Where did you get that coat you wore two weeks ago? The long one. Fantastic.

PIERRE: It wasn't too much?

ted: Don't ever stop. Fashion is something that has long been absent from the government scene.

PIERRE: Wonder why that is?

ted: They say that politics is showbiz for ugly people.

PIERRE: Who says that?

ted: When you get that many straight men in a large room, the style factor automatically plummets. Don't worry — it just makes you stand out even more. The ascot, the rose ... style is a way to introduce yourself without saying a word. Was that a leather suit I saw you in?

PIERRE: Spanish leather.

ted: I'd ask if you are really straight — but the sandals gave you away.

PIERRE: Too much?

ted: Maybe.

PIERRE: Maybe I should hire you as my stylist.

ted: Oh! Mr. Prime Minister! You flatter me. But you don't have the hips for any of my outfits. But I would love to suggest some things for your outfit for the debate.

PIERRE: As long as there's no headdress involved.

ted: Okay. Never mind then.

Sound: Federal Leader Debate TV intro. ted is in Vancouver, watching television.

ted: I've never watched a leadership debate before. But I've never had so much at stake before.

PIERRE: Leave all moral outrage aside for a moment and consider the waste: the tremendous waste of government resources, tracking people who are trying to be invisible, forcing them to report their friends, removing them from jobs, postings ... toppling them off of whatever precarious perch they had created for themselves.

And for what? Nothing good was accomplished. If nothing else, as a taxpayer you should be outraged.

ted: There he is. He looks so handsome next to Tommy Douglas, Stanfield, and that other French guy.

ANNOUNCER: *(voiceover)* Mr. Caouette: you stated that "The balance of power in parliament is more important than power itself."

If you were to obtain this balance of power, would you use it in order to block or facilitate the adoption of amendments to the criminal code which would allow homosexuality?

French lines are spoken aloud. The English translations follow as a voiceover.

CAOUETTE:

Je serai très franc.	I shall be very frank.
Dans le cas de	In the field of
l'homosexualité,	homosexuality
nous n'appuierons	it's clear we will not
pas le gouvernement.	support the government.
Cela créerait de	It would create
gros problèmes;	tremendous problems;
Ainsi, un homme —	since a man
pourrait marier	could marry
un autre homme —	another man,
cela créerait	this would create
des problems	problems
en ce qui concerne	for the maintenance
la pension	of the
alimentaire (ou l'entretien)	children who
des enfants nés	were born
de ces groupes.	of these groups.

ANNOUNCER: *(voiceover)* Mr. Stanfield.

STANFIELD: I also understand that the committee that's been considering the bill has had a good deal of difficulty concerning lack of information.

ANNOUNCER: *(voiceover)* Mr. Douglas.

DOUGLAS: Instead of treating it as a crime and driving it underground we ought to recognize it for what it is: it's a mental illness, it's a condition which ought to be treated by psychiatrists and social workers. We're not going to do this by throwing people into jail.

ANNOUNCER: *(voiceover)* Mr. Trudeau?

Again, the French lines are spoken aloud. The English translations follow as a voiceover.

TRUDEAU:	*Le projet de loi*	The bill doesn't
	ne se préoccupe pas de	deal with
	l'homosexualité;	homosexuality;
	il parle d'atteinte	it speaks of gross
	sexuelle.	indecency.
	Tout ce que nous avons	All we
	dit concernant	have said in
	l'amendement	the amendment
	est que ce qui se passe	is that what goes
	en privé	on in private
	entre deux	between two
	adultes consentants,	consenting adults,
	cela ne regarde qu'eux.	is their own business.

TRUDEAU: It isn't the police's business. It is the business of the Confessor. That is all there is to it. We are separating the idea of sin and the idea of crime.

Closing CBC theme music and the test pattern tone.

ted: That's why I would never make it in politics. I'm far too interesting.

He won. You know that, of course. Or I wouldn't be here. In all my Glory.

The real battle was still to come. And our new Prime Minister Pierre was fighting different battles, you know, as he became more involved with the government. We lost our easy access to him. We didn't get as many meetings as we used to. But he would still meet with us. And these were the times when we use to leave Vancouver and fly to Ottawa just for a two-hour meeting with this man. And think that we were privileged.

Because he was a magnificent man.

The Prime Minister' Office, Parliament Hill

ted: Parliament Hill is impressive in person. TV makes everything look so small.

PIERRE: It's good that you are able to see it for yourself. Makes it less ... abstract.

ted: It was either that or get a bigger TV. I have to say: election night, was the highlight of my life so far.

PIERRE: Did you actually watch the whole thing?

ted: Every second. We were all on the edge of our seat. And then there was a drag show after.

PIERRE: I wish I had seen that.

ted: I wish you had, too.

PIERRE: Well — let's raise that bar.

ted: I don't know — it was a pretty good drag show ...

I knew you would win. But thank you for winning. I felt like I finally had a say in the direction of my future.

PIERRE: It's not over. The bill has polarized the MPs. Are you really sure you want to see the debate?

ted: I wouldn't miss it.

PIERRE: It could go on for days.

ted: Then I'll probably miss most of it. Days? Really? I can't stay that long.

At this point, what could be left to say?

PIERRE: It's their last chance to condemn. They'll take every second they can.

ted: It should be televised.

PIERRE: Trust me — no one wants that.

There's been serious resistance — especially from Quebec.

ted: Lots of those men will never change their mind.

PIERRE: They saw the piles of mail arrive in their offices. It left them no choice but to pick a side. Let history judge them. We have a solid legal argument — even a political one — but it's the human stories that change minds.

You're going to hear lots of negative things in the debate.

ted: I know.

PIERRE: You really don't have to subject yourself to it.

ted: I've heard it all before.

PIERRE: In both official languages?

ted: That'll be new.

PIERRE: The vote is a formality. The bill will pass. Just think — in a few days ... you won't be breaking the law anymore.

Pause.

ted: Is that really true?

PIERRE: Excuse me?

ted: I've been thinking ... the way the amendment is phrased —

PIERRE: It's been through three readings —

ted: Nowhere does it say homosexuality is legal.

PIERRE: Because it was never illegal.

ted: So if it was never illegal, how does this change anything?

PIERRE: It's about gross indecency.

ted: Which is something that has always been open to interpretation.

PIERRE: We have clarified that definition.

ted: You've narrowed the scope slightly. I've been looking at what happened in Britain — the results aren't what they expected. They're still arresting queers. Even more than they used to.

It's so far from over. And suddenly ... I have the feeling that it's not going to be enough.

PIERRE: The bill is designed to protect what goes on in your bedroom. Your private life is no longer something you need to fear.

ted: But what about my public life? I'm not just gay when I'm having sex. The only way to stay safe is to keep it a secret. That defeats the whole point.

PIERRE: It will change everything eventually. In time.

ted: Society still hasn't made a legal space for us.

PIERRE: Politics is a long game.

ted: You're asking me to continue to tolerate being a second-class citizen.

Until when?

PIERRE: You said you're a very patient Queen.

ted: You know, I am always being told to be patient. I don't know how much longer I can do that. I don't want to go back to the hospital.

PIERRE: Back to the hospital?

ted: I've never told anyone this, but I'm living proof that no one suddenly turns straight after electroshock therapy. It was painful. It was humiliating. And it was utterly pointless.

PIERRE: When did this happen?

ted: In L.A. Dad came to rescue me. If he hadn't ...

I'm not sick. What's sick is this fucking world I live in.

Pause.

PIERRE: You can't stop now. You once told me that without a mission, life was worth nothing.

ted: Why do I feel impotent? If I was really the Empress of Canada, I'd issue a decree.

PIERRE: You had to know that this is only the beginning.

ted: You're new to this battle. I've been fighting for this for fifteen years already.

And after the bill passes? What then?

PIERRE: Your people can celebrate. This is the generation that can make the change happen.

ted: We need to be free in public. Where people can see.

PIERRE: This is just the first step.

ted: I know. And now I want more.

PIERRE: Then you need to go back into battle. We can't just legislate how people think.

ted: I don't know how much fight I have left in me.

PIERRE: I have a feeling you will continue to surprise yourself.

Are you sure you want to watch the debate?

ted: I'm here to see Question Period. The future of my Empire is at stake.

I'm assuming you arranged a throne for me.

PIERRE: I'll look up and see you in the visitors gallery tomorrow?

ted: I'll be the one waving.

PIERRE: The Royal Wave?

ted: You know me so well.

PIERRE: Now, I'm sorry to cut this short ...

ted: I understand. You're a busy man.

PIERRE: I know you flew all the way across the country —

ted: It was my pleasure.

PIERRE: Safe travels. Your Majesty.

ted: Oh ... Mr. Prime Minister ...

Montage. Both actors take turns playing the following politicians. A combination of actors and voiceovers may be used.

ANNOUNCER: The Honourable Member from Ottawa-Carleton, Minister of Justice

TURNER: Mr. Speaker, this legislation is the most important and all-embracing reform of the criminal and penal law ever attempted at one time in this country.

POLITICIAN 1: Once you legalize a disease you must legalize all others. That would be, Mr. Speaker, something utterly ridiculous.

POLITICIAN 2:

C'est un fait reconnu que	It is generally recognized
l'homosexualité est	that homosexuality is
une maladie, et parfois,	a disease, and sometimes
un vice.	a vice.

TURNER: Mr. Speaker, this bill takes a stand on some of the most controversial questions of our time.

POLITICIAN 3: This is a disgrace to the Canadian public. A government which relaxes the regulations and curbs on homosexuality is in the process of remaking our society.

POLITICIAN 4:

C'est la raison	That is the reason why
pour laquelle	I sincerely
je crois sincèrment,	believe,
Monsieur le Président,	Mr. Speaker,
que lacure pour	that the cure for
l'homosexualité	homosexuality
n'est pas la légalisation,	is not legalization,
mais plutôt est d'avoir	but rather
recours à des	recourse to
mesures préventives	preventive measures,
et à des soins	and to curative methods
curatifs pour	applying to the
les victimes de ce fléau.	victims of that evil.

TURNER: These amendments remove certain sexual conduct between consenting adults in private from the purview of criminal law.

POLITICIAN 5: This legislation permits homosexual acts in private between two consenting adults — no more than two. Apparently, for some reason, if there are more than two it becomes illegal. Three's a crowd.

POLITICIAN 6:

Je me demande,	I wonder,
Monsieur le Président,	Mr. Speaker,
si le gouvernement actuel,	if the present government
n'est pas l'instrument	is not simply the tool
d'un horrible complot	of a dreadful plot against
contre notre civilisation.	our civilization.

TURNER: Parliament, by not imposing the criminal law upon fornication or adultery is not thereby condoning fornication or adultery. Individuals will continue to be responsible to themselves for their moral behaviour.

POLITICIAN 7: I think it must be agreed, Mr. Speaker, that homosexuality is a psychological aberration.

POLITICIAN 8:

Avec l'amendement	With the amendment
concernant	regarding
l'homosexualité,	homosexuality,
on peut s'attendre	we can expect
à des mariages.	weddings.

POLITICIAN 9: Homosexuals are mostly inclined to pervert youngs ters and the Minister opens the door ever wider ...

POLITICIAN 10:

Les homosexuels	Homosexuals
sont probablement	are probably
des gens malades.	sick people.

POLITICIAN 11: Homosexuals prey on juveniles. It is something that spreads like a plague, for there is no more destructive drive than the sexual impulse running wild.

POLITICIAN 12: If homosexuality were practised on a widespread scale society would break down ... the human race would in a matter of time become extinct.

POLITICIAN 13: We are bringing the morals and values of skid row into the salons and drawing rooms of the nation...

POLITICIAN 14: Welcome to the destruction or even the suicide of society.

POLITICIAN 15: I do not want to have this kind of debauchery in our nation.

POLITICIAN 16: Do you want me to legalize sexual intercourse with the animals of Canada?

POLITICIAN 17: What has the government done for the people since December 13 last?

An MP interjects loudly: "Make them all homos!" A collective gasp. Pierre stands. The MPs go silent.

PIERRE: There is no such thing as a model or ideal Canadian. A society which emphasizes uniformity is one which creates intolerance and hate.

The past is to be respected and acknowledged, but not to be worshipped. It is our future in which we will find our greatness. Let us overthrow the totems, break the taboos. Or better, let us consider them cancelled. Coldly, let us be intelligent.

An outraged chorus of parliamentary desk-pounding and boos.

May 18, 1969. ted is in Vancouver, sitting in his living room. Pierre is in his office in Ottawa.

ted: I wonder if he will call.

PIERRE: It seemed only right to call.

ted: He'll be too busy.

PIERRE: To call someone who would truly understand what was at stake.

ted: I'm positive he'll be too busy.

PIERRE: And so I dialled the number.

ted: On to the next major issue. I'm sure.

PIERRE: Ringing.

ted: The phone rang. The phone call I had been waiting for.

PIERRE: Ringing.

ted: My whole life, really.

PIERRE: Ringing.

ted: I mean, even before I could imagine it, I dreamed it.

PIERRE: I let it ring.

ted: Nothing would ever be the same. I could almost taste the change.

PIERRE: I let it ring.

ted: I let it ring. I was in a state of suspension. I didn't want to answer the phone.

PIERRE: Surely he knows the vote was today.

ted: I didn't want this moment to end. This moment contained an endless future. I knew what today meant.

PIERRE: Maybe he's out celebrating.

ted: I didn't want to be around anyone for a little while. I wanted to savour the feeling of victory.

PIERRE: I'll let it ring a few more times.

ted: I just let it ring.

PIERRE: Someone needs to invent a machine that can take messages.

TED: Whatever it is, whoever is calling, will just have to wait.

PIERRE: What time is it in Vancouver anyway?

ted: Because I'm now a Canadian. In every sense of the word. I can finally feel it.

PIERRE: I would have thought —

ted: Okay, I'm ready. (*answers the phone*) Hello?

PIERRE: Congratulations, Your Majesty.

ted: Oh, Mr. Prime Minister!

PIERRE: We did it.

ted: Did we?

PIERRE: Yes. We did. I hope you feel that all your work —

ted: *Our* work.

PIERRE: It was time. Canada needed to move past the contradictions, the inconsistencies.

ted: Free to move in its own direction.

PIERRE: Do you feel equal?

ted: Not yet. But at least I can imagine what that could feel like now.

PIERRE: You're quite the Canadian, ted. You should be proud.

ted: I'm not sure I've earned pride yet. I've always been proud of my country ... always loved it ... but I still need to learn to trust it.

PIERRE: Trust takes time.

ted: I'm a very patient Queen.

PIERRE: Yes, you are. So what's next for you? What have you been waiting to do with your new freedom?

ted: The drag society. It's time for Vancouver to elect its first Empress. And I want to open a gay club.

So what's next for you? Oh, of course — you'll be running a country — busy, busy ... Don't you get lonely? I mean, you have a nation behind you. Most of a nation. Part of a nation. But no one beside you. You only have to ask. I'll be right there.

PIERRE: Calm down, Your Majesty.

ted: 'Twas not to be. Alas. Heavy lies the wig that wears the crown.

PIERRE: I should let you go.

ted: I never want this call to end.

PIERRE: And yet it must.

ted: I know.

PIERRE: It's been a pleasure working with you, ted.

ted: It's been a dream come true, Pierre. And I say that without a trace of superlative.

PIERRE: Good luck with everything. My Empress.

ted: Oh. Mister Prime Minister.

Dial tone.

ted: I held the phone to my ear for at least a half hour, listening to the dial tone. I replayed and imagined the conversation over and over, memorizing his voice, my replies ... this was the stuff of legend. How many drag queens could say that the prime minister had called them up to congratulate them?

One. Only one. That's how many.

ted slowly hangs up.

ted: So why didn't I feel like celebrating?

Because it was far from over.

The law had been grey. But now it was black and white. Our veil of secrecy was ripped away. We had operated under the radar for decades. Now we had to be accountable. Some of us were ready for that. But most of us were still living in fear. Peoples' minds don't just change because a bill was passed in parliament.

Pride isn't something that is legislated. It requires generations of learning how to think differently.

It was a new day. But it was the same Canada. Cruising the parks wasn't suddenly legal. Kissing your lover wasn't suddenly acceptable. George Everett Klippert didn't get out of prison for two more years — the last man jailed for homosexuality. Equality wasn't suddenly real. I still had to imagine it.

As summer began, Bill C-150 received Royal Assent, and was signed into law.

The very next day, a group of drag queens and trans-folk and dykes and homos cornered a bunch of police inside the Stonewall Inn in New York. The resulting riot lasted three days.

It barely made a ripple in the news. But those of us who heard about it through the queer grapevine knew what it meant. Finally, the fabric of our complacency had been torn. Finally, we know what to do.

It's not going to happen immediately. We have no idea how long it will take. But it's starting.

We're going to war. For you.

Many of us will die.

For you. For the nation you will inherit.

You'll inherit this battle too.

Revolution.

If I'm lucky, I'll live through it.

Slow fade to black.

ABOUT THE AUTHOR

Playwright, author, composer, Queer historian, and artistic director of Guys In Disguise, Darrin Hagen has created more than forty plays and written dozens of articles illuminating Queer history.

His plays include *The Edmonton Queen*, the Sterling-nominated *The Empress & The Prime Minister*, *Witch Hunt at the Strand*, *10 Funerals*, and *Buddy*, as well as *Tornado Magnet: A Salute to Trailer Court Women*, *Go West Young Man*, *Metronome*, and the international hit *BitchSlap!*. His holiday comedy *With Bells On* has been produced in Ireland, Virginia, and Florida and was adapted into a musical by New York City's Live and In Color, with a world premiere in 2023 at Theatre Network.

Darrin wrote, directed, and composed for the award-winning 2024 feature-length documentary *Pride vs. Prejudice: The Delwin Vriend Story*, which has been screened across Canada, the United States, and Europe. He was awarded the 2025 Edmonton Film Prize for his cinematic debut.

He has so far won seven Sterling awards (and received more than forty nominations) for his work in theatre, as well as multiple AMPIA awards. He was inducted into the Q Hall of Fame Canada, was listed as one of the 25 Most Influential Alberta artists in the last 25 years, was named one of 100 Edmontonians of the Century, and was cited as one of "Six Who Inspire" by Edify magazine.

Darrin lives in Edmonton with his husband Kevin, their Boston Terrier, and, for a few months of the year, a lush garden.

PRAIRIE PLAY SERIES

Far As the Eye Can See — Paul Thompson and RudyWiebe
Davin: The Politician — Ken Mitchell
Prairie Performance — ed. Diane Bessai
Blood Relations and Other Plays — Sharon Pollack
Showing West: Three Prairie Docu-Dramas — ed. Diane Bessai and Don Kerr
Eight Plays For Young People: Prairie Performance II — Joyce Doolittle
NeWest Plays by Women — ed. Diane Bessai and Don Kerr
Deverell of the Globe — Rex Deverell
Plays at the Iron Bridge, or The Autobiography of Tom Horror — Wilfred Watson
Rebels in Time — Ken Mitchell
The Hungry Spirit and Other Plays — Elsie Park Gowan
The Wolf Plays — Brad Fraser
The Ugly Man — Brad Fraser
Poor Superman: A Play with Captions — Brad Fraser
Love and Human Remains — Brad Fraser
Ethnicities — ed. Anne Nothof
The Aberhart Summer: A Play — David Massing
Scraping the Surface — Lyle Victor Albert
NextFest Anthology — Glenda Stirling
Snake in Fridge — Brad Fraser
Naked at School: Plays for Teens — Chris Craddock
A Teatro Trilogy — Stewart Lemoine
The Room With Five Walls — Byrna Barclay
NextFest Anthology II: Plays from the Syncrude Next Generation — Steve Pirot
At the Zenith of the Empire — Stewart Lemoine
Metastasis and Other Plays — Gordon Pengilly
Harvest and Other Plays — Ken Cameron
Witness to a Conga — Ken Cameron
Martini with a Twist — Clem Martini
Public Speaking and Other Plays — Chris Craddock
Dear Johnny Deere — Ken Cameron
The Mighty Carlins and Other Plays — Collin Doyle
Matara: The Elephant Play — Conni Massing

This book has been typeset in Garamond and Futura.
Written, edited, designed, printed, and published
by humans in Canada.